Ex Nihilo

Seth Masek

ISBN: 978-0999871232

Into deep space our visions cast,

reflecting back luminous past

Table of Contents

Chapter 1: Judgment

Deep space

Deep space
Artifact
Relic of an alien past
Brought back to earth
Pioneers
Gone for one too many years

Masses
Blindly laude
Proof of science, reproof God
What they ignored
In plain sight
Evil stowed away in flight

Released
Infected
A terror resurrected
His will unleashed
Mastery
Darkness and divinity

Spores loosed
Indwelling
Cruel, wicked deeds compelling

Lacking answers

Denial

Many guilty, none on trial

Impeached

Arrested

God's faithful, all suspected

Superstition

Reversal

Genocide's dress rehearsal

Falsehood

First evil

Black gems to please the Devil

Violent delights

Ends to end

Earth's reward, the fruits of sin

Deep space

Artifact

Returned us our inglorious past

Denying truth

Consequence

Hopeless those who won't repent

Empty town

There is a town, far out of town
Overgrown, deserted ground
Toxic rivers now run dry
Baked under an atomic sky

Center bare, there mill no people
None to praise beneath the steeple
A faithful flock no more crammed in
The house of God so long abandoned

A traveler in dusty robes
Found this town off long dirt road
His purpose solely that his own
Two blades of steel to him sown

Donned in black, yet not he priestly
When Wormwood fell, he was set free
As the star burned through the sky
His captors knew the time was nigh

From the mountains he descended
As the world around them ended
The last chance of humanity
A demon's heart, barbarity

Death to death, but not to ash
Black blood rained as lightning crashed
His blades cut clean through rotted bones
Clipping skulls like rolling stones

Upon the bricks his bloodied feet
Danced upon the bloodied street
In undead flesh had he been drenched
Yet not the traveler's thirst was quenched

In this town, far out of town
Dwelt greater evil underground
A paragon of evil stirred
Its minions' cries above it heard

Beneath the church came an eruption
Burst forth the source of this corruption
Its two black horns stretched forth like fangs
From pools of venom the traveler sprang

Lava eyes bled fire in showers
Night turned to day by their dark power
Yet fear gripped not the traveler's heart
For black it was as his counterpart

The beast had thick and armored skin
No human weapon could it rend
But the traveler's spectral blades could pierce
The beast became all more the fierce

The demon seed spread its onyx claws
As poison dripped from its jagged maw
The hooded wretch drew forth his blades
And to the epic fight engaged

The war they fought spanned an epoch
An endless night of flame and rock
Of equal strength and no clear weakness
Was there no end to the bleakness?

They danced in blurs of steel and black
The warrior leapt to the demon's back
His two blades sank into its hide
The beast it writhed, the beast it cried

The beast staggered on its cloven hooves
Black blood poured through the steel grooves
And just before the beast did yield
Its venom struck the traveler's heel

The beast's volcanic skin went dim
This traveler had banished him
Back to hell had it retired
To rot within the lake of fire

As evil fell there came a breeze
The traveler fell upon his knees
The poison pumped within his veins
No time had he on earth to reign

His captors when they saw this feat
Descended they to savior greet
And had they in their power to cure
Their protector must endure

So saved they him who passed the test
And put him into endless rest
For if evil were to be reborn
Awake he must to fight the scorn

The world returned into a state
Where darkness no longer our fate
The undead returned to the earth
The birds filled springtime air with mirth

And in the town, far out of town

It was rebuilt out of the ground

The roads were cleaned, the buildings white

The people's faces oh so bright

Looked they up to the mountain

And blessed the priestly, prepared men

For they now knew how to defend

You slay the devil with a demon

Seven days until my death

Seven days until my death
My tormentors watch every breath
These cold, black, lifeless, jagged stones
Compound my cries like microphones

Six days now until my death
My throat is coarse, my path is set
A darkness seeps into my soul
My suffering is someone's goal

Five days now until my death
This evil clearly won't regret
Descent to madness as I starve
I rot within this stony jar

Four days now until my death
This solitude becomes a gift
Bloodthirsty eyes have left me be
To ponder my captivity

Three days left until my death
I try to make the sunlight stretch
Salvation in a hole above
Have shred my hands without a glove

Two days left until my death
And for the few hours that I've slept
Girded by my resolution
Suffering my absolution

One day now until my death
My skin, it shivers, and it sweats
Folded hands for the first time pray
To be avenged on judgment day

Now the day upon my death
Cold hands take me by the neck
Staring at an empty basket
That will now become my casket

Your pain gives me purpose

Your pain, it gives me purpose
Your doubts, they give me faith
Your calling out for saving
Is your one redeeming grace

Your cause, it has no meaning
Your will, it holds no weight
Your need to so be needed
Keeps you locked behind a gate

Your cries, they bring me joy
Your tears, a soothing balm
Your passion for attention
Is the hardest thing to calm

Your weakness makes me confident
Your dreams prove but a farce
Your wanting to be wanted by
A man who has no heart

Sulfur island

Limbs like leaves trembled in the wind

A frontline strong but soon to end

No coward stood within the ranks

Though all were sailing on death's plank

After days of ceaseless rain

The cool dry air portended pain

Had this been a day without war

This tiny island would they have adored

The star that lights the morning sky

The last night in so many eyes

The rocking decks made sickly haste

To the beach their bloodied flesh would paint

And as the shallow waters arrived

Thousands of bees began to sting the sides

These little boxes driving souls

With weapons bare and death the goal

When battle cries rang out so fierce

The steel door fell and lead did pierce

Before the triggered fingers blinked

Ten-thousand rifles to ground did sink

The front line crumpled to the floor

The second wave over them bore

And flesh like hills did start to heap

No hellcats could bring them relief

Enemy daggers from mountain high

Bulwarked the stone from every side

The ocean blue was no retreat

To not push on would mean defeat

In hours like years the tide would turn

The dead no time to bury or burn

This sulfur island wrought with rot

Survivors few for what they fought

Bodies strewn about like rags

Through smoke and ash, they raised a flag

What is the price for victory?

Six-thousand, eight-hundred slain Marines

They say

They say a man was born from dust
He starts to learn as his mind rusts
To be uncertain is a must
If one's to see beneath the crust

They say a man learned in a cave
A billion souls, his words may save
A thousand years since his conclave
The dust still settles on his grave

They say a man the world did change
By setting sail to land so strange
And from the fowl not in a cage
All life from not, a causeless wage

There is no sum, there is no gain
When all the answers sound the same
Conviction lies with the insane
The only truth is found in pain

And soon the darkness

And soon the vials

Overcoming

All are running

No help coming

And soon the madness

Overpowered

All are cowards

Trampled flowers

And soon the darkness

Unchained sorrow

Blindness follows

No tomorrow

Tower grey

The tower grey will never sway
Its foundation cannot wilt away
For within the vast sea of strong stones
Rests a thousand years of kingly bones

Ten-thousand candles dress the halls
The warming light makes bright the walls
A scholar's sojourn in the study
Makes the mind both quick and steady

But though it seems invincible
The dense is still destructible
For stalking lions roam outside
From within all pure hearts hide

And knights in chain withstand the pain
They suffer though their souls unstained
Sentinels standing by each night
To keep the keep and fight the fight

An epoch of spirituality
Shaped steel advanced technology
Distracted not by frivolities
Short years make sure priorities

Puzzle

The board is split into disconnected pieces
No time to solve but no time to walk away
Another day, no closer to the answer
Another day, one more chance to walk away

Not every day will manifest a purpose
The seal is broken, there's no secrets anymore
Another day, no closer to the answer
Another day, one more chance to walk away

There isn't always a way
When there's no time but a day
The stage is torn down
There's nowhere left to play
There isn't always a way
Sometimes all it takes is a day
Turn it upside down
And let it drift away

The puzzle is not one meant to be solved
If it were, there'd be no roads left to explore
Another day, no closer to the answer
Another day, one more chance to walk away

Witching hour

There is power in the witching hour
When sleep and conscious war
Slayer of dreams before they meet the page
These fleshy drapes, they pull such weight
Battle scars the only joy

There is power in the witching hour
Sleep lurking in the dark
Do not allow thy mind's eye blink
Do not thy limbs make rest on the soft
Capture now what fills thy soul

There is power in the witching hour
Prowling thief of inspiration
Flee from the fields and roaming herds
Let loose the pen, let chaos reign
Expect not to have this chance again

There is power in the witching hour
Before the conscious sublimates
Capture what stands out in the night
While weary souls recapture strength
Late hours be thine only break

Venom

It's invisible in water
Once you drink it, you'll be calmer
Slowly drifting in the slipstream
You won't want to wake from this dream

What magic from her potions arise?
Take another drink between her skies
Not all poison should an ailing man despise
Taste the venom bleeding from her eyes

It's impossible not to wander
As the fluid makes you stronger
There is not a safe place to hide
From the tears that have not yet dried

And from her cup I'm sipping again
The drug is dripping, seeping within
The venom's quickly taking control
Injected when she holds me, by her touch I will fold

What magic from her potions arise?
Take another drink between her skies
Not all poison should a sickly man despise
Taste the venom bleeding from her eyes

Forward march

Forward march

Do not stop

When they fly

Some will drop

Forward march

Do not yield

Breach the front

Burn the field

Forward march

Show no fear

Do not say

Surrender

Serpent

It spawned from where few footsteps tread

The whispers of a faceless dread

And before they could seize control

The legion had gained a foothold

The demic quickly spread to pan

And within months were few to stand

No wealth or station spared the soul

The reaper's coffers overflowed

The race to cure befell by curse

This creature could not tech reverse

The ghost swept plains a testament

Of how quickly man can fragment

Those who survived had passed the test

Immune to death that took the rest

But comfort could not one heart take

Our mother did our spirits break

Our War

The tide bleached red
More boots splash down
The smell of rot
As thunder sounds

The broken air
By whistling fate
A purposed charge
Toward victory's gate

No penman's craft can capture
No preacher's words will rapture
All that suffer share the price
All that fell to sacrifice

Our war was not our choice
In death we don't rejoice
Our way we made our own
By sorrow is our bravery shown

The billowed black
Signaled afar
The stripes would stand
As would our stars

The canvas green

The war-torn soil

Unsullied souls

Not seeking spoils

No penman's craft can capture

No preacher's words will rapture

All that suffer share the price

All that fell to sacrifice

Our war was not our choice

In death we don't rejoice

Our way we made our own

By sorrow is our bravery shown

The splintered hearts

Which saw friends fall

Out of the mire

Stood they tall

Returned to freedom

Bound to the past

Remember them

If we are to last

Looking up from underneath

Looking up from underneath
Through the shadows and the deep
Nothing firm like first belief
As we had in our young years

It is not safe when we retreat
The weak, they fade out and deplete
No use to pray or run away
Our dreams will not recover

Looking up from underneath
Trampled by the cold and heat
Bodies strewn across the street
So much pain, so much hunger

It is not safe when we retreat
The weak, they fade out and deplete
Whether we stay or turn away
Our dreams will not recover

Looking up from underneath
When every argument will cease
Threatened by the same disease
As that of our fathers

It is not safe when we retreat

The weak, they fade out and deplete

What do we say the scales weigh?

Our dreams will not recover

If not, then what

Is it not a miracle if it's happened before?

Is a secret paranoia if one's not really sure?

Will our car run out of gas if we are sitting indoors?

Will it count as sacrifice if that is what's adored?

Sit and see, patiently, between two mirrors lies the
    edge of eternity

Pick up the phone, but don't call home—accept that
    you are all alone

If not then what, if not then who; it all has boiled
    down to you

If not then what, if not then who; if you believe it,
    then it's true

Is a problem complicated if it cannot be solved?

Is a mind prone agitated if it's not evolved?

Will discord turn malcontent if it cannot be resolved?

Will the king's prose turn to poison when nobody's
    involved?

Cross the sea with bravery, embrace the power of
    impurity

Turn the tide, it's bona fide—the more you rend the
    less you've tried

If not then what, if not then who; it all comes down
    to what you do

If not then what, if not then who...repent, repeat,
    return, redo

Dry wood

Dry wood, white like a field of bones, lies slain upon
the desert floor

Casualties of a war before the men who birth them
have been born

A thousand years pass by, and no season shifts the
dust and dry

No soul hears the battle cry of buzzards balking in
the sky

One million runs around the sun when every beast
gargantuan

The earth beneath their feet undone, these epic relics
had their fun

Populations like constellations lighting up the
mountain's trough

Vainglory is the only story when witless time defeats
all thought

Lightning rod

You mix it up to make a splash
Then wear attention like a rash
You stir the pot; ignored, you pout
You say it loud to mask your doubt

You live like a lightning rod
You're ordinary being odd
No opinion being broad
If it's not yours, it is a fraud

You miss the subtle every day
Pontificating to convey
What you may or may not believe
Assuming all try to deceive

There is no day you are not on
A donkey to the water drawn
You can't relax and want to share
That if you think it, we should care

You live like a lightning rod
You're ordinary being odd
No opinion being broad
If it's not yours, it is a fraud

It is necessary to impart

That lightning rods still play a part

For they run deep into the earth

Assuring no lightning can hurt

Refuge are you from a storm

Taking on what causes harm

So thank you for being flawed

All of us need a lightning rod

Have you ever

Have you ever had a moment that made you feel
   insignificant?

Or made you think your life isn't relevant?

All your decisions are just made for the hell of it?

Have you ever been on the wrong side of disparity?

No matter how hard you focus, there's no clarity

That faith, hope, love are the ultimate rarity

Sometimes I feel unlovable

And none of my problems solvable

Every dream I have is impossible

Finding any joy, implausible

Have you ever felt for nothing you are reverent?

That in your life only the wrong choices are
   prevalent?

And any clever thing you do is but a parlor trick

Have you suffered through and struggled with
   insanity?

And felt the only thing you protect is your vanity

That every smile which you muscle is momentary

Sometimes I feel unlovable

And none of my problems solvable

Every dream I have is impossible

Finding any joy, implausible

I don't expect you to understand my silence

Though I'm calm outside, inside of me is violence

This depression is a wave that is relentless

I don't ever think I'll come back to my senses

Sometimes I feel unlovable

And none of my problems solvable

Every dream I have is impossible

Finding any joy, implausible

In a land that breathes

In a land that breathes
Dragon fire from below
The earth, she seethes
As she makes mountains grow

As the steam erupts
And the rocks slide down
One cannot interrupt
As water splits the ground

On a land beasts roam
Safe from sinning hands
New world but old home
Ancients stood for what she stands

This little light

This little light was once so bright
It stayed the night and fought the fight
This little light was once so new
It saw me through and kept me true

This little light of mine divine
Was once so fine, now in decline
This little light of mine glows faint
Embrace the taint and slay the saint

This little light was once so bright
Now say goodnight, the wrong is right
This little light was once so new
A dismal hue in which I rue

Line

A little line beneath the brine

Just deep enough where no light shines

A little string that ends in death

To bind its prey within depth

The meal false, detect the ruse

For those who don't will surely lose

Asking not, could feast cause harm?

Hunger consumes a piercing barb

Another fool fell for the food

The hunter's victory oh so crude

Drawn from the blue and crashing wake

To a world which suffocates

Tributary

Drift along a tributary
Flowing at the river's pace
The jungle heat is quite contrary
No winter's bite has found this place

The deadwood safe when sewn with reeds
With careful hands, no water bleeds
The craft a craft of which is worthy
Exploring worlds upon the thirsty

Navigate each seamless bend
What new wonders will she send?
The water dim but holds much life
A testament to balanced strife

The safety net of calm is faux
As fowl and beast foresee
Nature's wrath will take in tow
A witless wanderer out to sea

Soldier

Moving toward a bleak horizon
Marching toward the battleground
Murder now the path of mercy
Reaping souls and spirits make

Cartridge locked and fully loaded
Confidence in their instruments
Graves the rest they grant their foemen
Agents of God's wrath in the flesh

Grace is not the faithful answer
Grace is not a saving force
Steel and lead portend our mercy
Even as the atoms loose

Ending all the sedentary
Bayonets for those of sloth
Combing through the faceless masses
Giving up won't give them back

Atop the crown, a twirling dagger
They nettle those that cross their path
Hide well or face the thirsty iron
Nothing spared and nothing saved

Children of brutality

Temple maidens in white linens
Bathing dignitary bones
Quartered marble draped in sinners
Ivy grown by paupers' blood

Fabled times, as history teaches
Remembered by the ancient tomes
Statues stand for the worst of our species
Our children worship wicked ones

If past is prologue, what are we?
But students of their history
If barbaric they, then what are we?
But children of brutality

Epic battles, arcing lines
Famous quotes of Sophist minds
All now tread upon by weakness
Cowards starve where valor dined

The greatest warrior of old
Was but a child when kingship fell
The lion's prophet had foretold
He wept—what more is there to tell?

If past is prologue, what are we?

But students of their history

If barbaric they, then what are we?

But children of brutality

Fire princess

A world turned dark and ruled by fear
A time with little hope or cheer
A realm of warmth turned realm of snow
A curse a wicked witch bestowed

Stonework once in sunlight shone
Stonework now dulled and windblown
The royal keep entombed in ice
For wealth and glory, this was the price

Citizens once so full of life
Now were bound to chill and strife
By widowed queen who sold her soul
To a wicked witch, for whom she toiled

The widowed queen had selfish been
The widowed queen knew not but sin
Her subjects all believed her lie
Her best-kept secret, regicide

Then queen sought out so many ways
To store up gold and buy her praise

Although her people sought not war
The widowed queen kept wanting more

Her kingdom spread from sea to sea
Until the world fell at her feet
No enemies could borders breach
One enemy could her heart reach

Creeping upon every breath
A stopper must she put in death
And so her mind went mad to wild
The widowed queen offered her child

To the dark she cried for trade
One life betrayed for one life saved
Out to the winds her prayer soared
And in the shadows evil stirred

For in the kingdom dwelt a hag
A witch whose dwelling was a crag
She was a master of dark art
But she could not a family start

The witch had lived so many years
To extend her life she'd need an heir
A child whose soul she could replace
A child with whom she would trade place

A special child must it be
Their blood be born from royalty
So when the queen called out that night
The witch's ravens took to flight

When learned the witch, the evil witch
When learned she of this plan to switch
Crafted she elixir three
One life, one death, one slavery

Forward sent the witch her word
Upon the wings of a black bird
A message to convince the queen
Her child for long life guaranteed

Pause we must, for it is just
The young princess we must discuss
The kingdom only knew her name
For the queen alone wanted fame

Her name was short, but very strong

The kind you'd put into a song

Her face was kind, her heart was free

This spotless creature named Marie

A little dreamer full of wishes

Fair skin dressed in angel's kisses

A brilliant girl with bright red hair

Was to the witch to be her heir

Whenceforth the witch met with the queen

To execute their evil scheme

Each did drink their own elixir

The queen soon knew the witch had tricked her

For crumpled she upon the floor

Her eyes now staring at death's door

The witch she cackled and then changed

A younger woman she became

The witch's wrinkles went away

As did her warts and hefty legs

Stealing life from her little slave

The princess ran but felt the pain

Marie could hear the witch's voice

The sound of evil had rejoiced

A perfect plan to steal the throne

Returning life to ancient bones

The witch then turned the world to ice

Her subjects forced to pay the price

The evil witch now ruled with fear

And tore down all that they held dear

The princess locked in tallest spire

Was hungry, cold, and oh so tired

For months she lived up there alone

Pain and loneliness her home

The spell so simple yet so cruel

The witch was stealing Marie's youth

And one day in that spire dark

A brilliant light before her sparked

Such a strange and shiny thing

Out of the light there stood a king

A vessel strong and oh so bright

His voice said, "It will be all right"

The princess thought that she had died
Then said the voice, "Come by my side"
The king whispered into her ear
"Look inside, your strength is near"

Suddenly he disappeared
And no longer did Marie fear
She stood and wiped the tears away
To her father's light she prayed

And in the dark her hair did glow
Her power grew in the shadows
Deep in her heart, no longer pain
The witch's power no longer drained

And came a cry from the great hall
"Where did all my power go?"
The witch, she called out for her slave
Her spell she needed to be saved

The minions brought her from the spire
As the evil witch perspired
She felt the age now coming back
Her spell was under an attack

But when Marie approached the witch
Her body flames, but clothes not singed
The minions ran from her in fear
The witch begged that she not draw near

"What spell is this that gives you might?"
The witch asked full of loathing fright
"What spell is this that set you free?"
The aging witch fell to her knees

No response did Marie share
Her pain did perfect magic bare
Balls of flame were in her hands
She smote the witch to blasted lands

Without a word, the world was freed
Marie released her energy
The kingdom that was once so bleak
Now saw the sun and felt the heat

Marie had all her magic spent
Mercy now her armament
The people crowned their newfound queen
And built the kingdom of their dreams

Today the people live in peace

The good princess will never cease

To make the best of all her days

And warm all hearts by her kind ways

Who would ever follow me?

I've tried one thousand times
Cried until my eyes fell out
Left it out for all to see
Who would ever follow me?

This is something new
No matter where I go
I will be connected to you
This is something new
I'm lost on Broadway
Wandering these rows for you

My universe within
Prison or absolution
Letter of hypocrisy
Who would ever follow me?

Loneliness sweet respite
Act of kindness selfishness
Error by rapidity
Who would ever follow me?

This is something new

No matter what I seek

All my paths lead back to you

This is something new

I've turned a corner

After I got lost in you

Wars we've fought

For all of the wars we've fought
Will we have the heart to win them?
For all the men we've lost
Will we have the strength to save them?
For all the bombs we've dropped
Will we have the will not to use them?

Forgive and forgotten, the blood of our fallen
What hope we had now torn asunder
I promise you this, you promised us that
And gave us a fate from which there is not
  repentance

For so many prayers we've bound
Will we have the faith to free them?
For so many lands we've taken
Will we have the courage to leave them?
For so many laws we've passed
Will we have the constitution to abide them?

Forgive and forgotten, the blood of our fallen
What hope we had now torn asunder
I promise you this, you promised us that
And gave us a fate from which there is not
  repentance

Turn away

As a child, I was sworn
To ways which weren't my own
I thought alone I'd bare the truth
Be the sinews when the worldly frayed
While they all played, I knelt and prayed
To a god who wasn't home

And now it's time to turn away
No warriors left to guard this town
And now it's time to turn away
The fiery hearts have all been drowned

Every night, my sleep
Nightmares into my dreams would creep
To pass the test and be the best
I'd sacrifice more than all the rest
Deep in my soul
Though I paid the toll
The beasts could I not defeat

And now it's time to turn away
No warriors left to guard this town
And now it's time to turn away
The fiery hearts have all been drowned

Requiem

Requiem for a long-lost love

Falling far, far from above

Listless feathers on the wind

Prove that time is not our friend

Dark skies surround the golden plains

Affixed to ground in windblown rain

Requiem for childhood friends

Our promises sure to rescind

All our lives are winding down

Until beneath six feet of ground

Fierce and true though Spartans be

What hope in their nobility?

Requiem for those that preach

Seeking truth beyond their reach

Quills and papyrus, ancient ink

Clasping chains on all that think

Books of scholars spread more lies

And in their pages our hope dies

The devil came down tonight

The devil came down tonight
I saw him taking out the light
You'll only fear when he's outside
You must let him fulfill your pride

The devil came down tonight
I heard his wings tear through the night
There's no need to pray, you'll see
Why drive out what sets you free?

The devil came down tonight
His fiery arms wrapped round me tight
What's a lifetime after all?
I'll answer to my master's call

Why, poet?

Why must poets write mystique?
Abstract the truth with wordy feats
No safe passage through their mind
Beware the stateless realm they bind

Why must poet pines grow long?
They still can't sing the sparrow's song
Launch dull arrows, quivers bare
So much prose their sorrows share

Why must poets vex the wise?
Lift the plains into the skies
Illusion is their mastery
We marvel in their mystery

To her altar

To her altar I was called
Be torn in two above the coal
The ritual, habitual
A flawless shrine for her sacrifice

At her altar I succumb
My throat is cut, my limbs go numb
There is no pain as I am drained
For the first time I can feel my heart

From her altar I'm prepared
The flames engulf, my secrets bare
No recompense, no remittance
In a sea of blood, I have been freed

As above, so below

As above, so below
Evil stirs beneath the borough
Locals warn, there dare not go
Where demons lurk in the shadows

As above, so below
Explore death's sanctum arms in tow
Whispers from the dead echo
Crippling those whose fear it shows

As above, so below
Sojourn not there all alone
Spirits fill corrupted souls
Turning friends into foe

As above, so below
Icy fingers grip the throat
Consume the soul as they choke
To enter was to forsake hope

Although no

Although no man be perfect
Although no man be pure
Despite that rip-torn feature
Long be gone be full

Although no mind be spotless
Although no mind be sure
Against which no weight tethers
The thought be sought grandeur

Although no voice be timeless
Although no voice be heard
Shifting sands and tides of war
Relent lest devils stir

On the sea

Far out at sea one fateful night
A dreadnaught sailed on waters bright
The moon was whole, it beamed and blazed
Flames licked the water, nature crazed

Winds they wailed and waves they crashed
Upon the hull the bright waves smashed
Just out to sea, beyond sight's reach
An evil burst forth from the deep

The captain saw the storm beyond
An omen on the sea there spawned
The captain did not change their course
The war they fled, he reasoned worse

Moonlight faded into blackness
Storm clouds filled the ocean's vastness
The haunted air carried a chill
And in a blink the sea stood still

And with the lateness of the hour
The captain's constitution cowered
Seamen awoke to his alarm
All hands on deck, they were a swarm

They manned their stations in a blur
All cannons poised and guns secured
A thunderous roar came from the sea
Belaying the tranquility

Then lightning lit the frigid air
Across the crew swept searing fear
Armed with every weapon drawn
Into the tempest dreadnaught drawn

Thunder splintered silent moments
Black rain bled forth like a torrent
Each needle prick brought stinging pain
Warm blood froze in the sailors' veins

Minutes passed like painful hours
Beaten by the heavy showers
Yet no soul gave way to this grief
Their hearts beat strong from their belief

Emerged they all from maw of war
They felled their foes as they did fall
Each bound to one as two forged rods
With love of country, faith in God

A sudden ripple through the air
The sea arose and then appeared
Scaled armor, impossibly dense
Lined with spears, a daggered fence

Upon the spine where acres spread
Sat there atop twelve dragon heads
Emerald eyes with golden rings
Twelve dueling heads spread out like wings

Its gleaming eyes ignored the ship
To it no more than harmless blip
Opal teeth in dark shone brightly
Serpent tongues struck out like lightning

"What is this we have fell upon?"
Replied captain, "Leviathan!"
Released he then the battle cry
Bright bullets lit the midnight sky

Cannons roared, lead whirred and blazed
But tracers proved they could not faze
Such massive thing, a foot an inch
Despite the wounds it did not flinch

Pain though dull, fierce sounds alerted
To ship's hull its eyes diverted
Kraken skulls converged, surrounded
Questioning what its hide had pounded

All the men abandoned stations
Fleeing evil's aberration
Deep black pupils locked on the crew
Then suddenly all the heads withdrew

Three bright lights filled falling sky
Followed they by twelve sets of eyes
Into black ocean fell the orbs
Then there arose a shimmering sword

The ship ignored, the beast withdrew
Emerged from hiding came the crew
Upon the deep, standing with sword
The captain cried, "Our savior, Lord!"

Eyes full of fire, long robes of white
An angel stood, ready to fight
Sword in his hand and shield in tow
The serpent cackled and bellowed

"Who defies me?" cried its voice
The demon spoke, battle its choice
No reply did the angel give
But raised his sword and bowed his head

A moment quiet, passed like hours
Suddenly they unleashed their powers
A stream of flame from beast shot forth
Angelic shield drawn out, absorbed

The clever creature changed its tact
With black acid it did attack
The angel's shield dissolved in hand
It melted to the sea like sand

The demon spoke, "Your faith is weak"
Then rose the angel to his feet
He drew his sword, his eyes wet gold
The dreadnaught crew watched this unfold

With no defense, the serpent struck
Twelve poisoned jaws to angel trucked
With swiftness of a cheetah's sprint
The angel's sword did two skulls split

His wings spread wide, his sword untamed
Ten vicious heads spit oil and flame
Despite the angel's speed and grace
This demon owned the earthly space

With malice of the devil's mind
Dark venom left the angel blind
Fire-worn robes and each wing broken
Viscous blood his sword was soaked in

With nothing left to him defend
The massive creature did descend
The ten remaining heads look pleased
"Your time has come," the demon teased

Then called the captain to his crew
"We must defend, our God is true!"
No weapons drew they out to fight
Instead they prayed into the night

"The Lord my shepherd, I shall not want"
The beast ignored, its prey to taunt
"The heavens declare the glory of God"
"The Lord my shield, my hope, my rod"

Each prayer and hymn to God implored

A cry for the angel restored

Just before death's consummation

The angel received his salvation

Sparks of bright lights as a shield

Instantly the angel was healed

The demon choked and did recoil

This angel would not be his spoil

A chorus of faithful men did praise

The God whom their angel did raise

And with a swift and mighty blow

The angel's sword sent ten below

Twitching necks to sea fell limply

Massive hulk of beast sank quickly

Before the angel disappeared

Surveyed the crew with crystal tears

Without a word the angel flashed

Back to the heavens his soul had dashed

The sky it split, the sea it calmed

A warm sun to the men a balm

With haste the ship fell back on course

From guilt of sin they had divorced

They learned the power of hope that sings

And faith in God grant angels' wings

Island

Matters not the setting, I can find no peace

Ocean, jungle, rocks sweating, falling from the cliffs

Happiness is not manufactured

For those who try, their lives be fractured

it here I alone, here alone

I know one thing sure, I know it well

None other need to see me through this world

Joy a youthful treasure, lost to aging seas

She was the one I've been after

Sailing seven seas, seven seas

Love must exist, if you believe it hard enough

To the emptiness I abdicate my energy

Enjoy the brief, compete with grief

It slips and dips as all belief

I break for no one, for no one

Commandment

If we live by the commandment
Will it save or will it damn us?
That God is love and image we
Are we eternity?
Or wasted energy?

Obeying the commandment
To love what neighbors hand us
It's hard to see and to conceive
That prayer sets us free
Should we so believe?

Taking life for the commandment
Death satisfies their own wrath
Without their weapons, convert none
No peace under the sun
The servant's heart they shun

Lay down life for the commandment
No greater form of payment
One debt was paid for many saved
Proved by an empty grave
My heart forever changed

Many trials may befall us

Be it rain, or sunshine, or just

A scar to show he marked us

May our souls be set loose

Whatever path we choose

Into me, a void

Breaking in, a void came creeping

Seeping in while I was sleeping

Taking my heart for the reaping

Shaking while my eyes were weeping

In a world of monsters, madness

Can light pierce a soul of blackness?

Sinners proved by their steadfastness

Devotees of death and sadness

Bleak and blurry, wings of fury

Ailed by that which should have cured me

Dancing flames to sea have lured me

Impaled upon the horns of purity

Is this the life our God intended?

Wills of men are oft pretended
Purpose known not, or contended
Wisdom's schoolyard unattended
Is this the life our God intended?

Faith a force hailed as resplendent
Truth and conviction, independent
Belief from reason hangs suspended
Is this the life our God intended?

We are not, cannot, will not change
Some just accept because it's strange
Scholars doubts born from their rage
Is all this from what stars arrange?

Poor from the rich go undefended
Greed and guile, evil bookended
Crimes, but no one apprehended
Is this the life our God intended?

Gravity makes straight light bended
Poets make the pain seem splendid
No soul knows whom they've offended
Is this the life our God intended?

Into a pit

Into a pit an angel fell
A gulf of coal and steel
Into a pit the angel fell
Armed with sword and shield

Into a pit an angel fell
His power all but drained
Into a pit the angel fell
With evil unrestrained

The angel fell, the angel fell
With evil by his side
The angel called out in the depth
For light to be his guide

Into a pit an angel fell
Steel cords wrapped he round
Into a pit the angel fell
The demon had he bound

Into a pit an angel fell
The trench become a tomb
Into a pit the angel fell
Creating evil's womb

The angel fell, the angel fell

The evil he endured

The angel crawled out of the depth

The enemy secured

Soul piercer

Mortals dare not linger here
In a place they've learned to fear
Mortals dare not there trespass
Where the darkness comes so fast

Mortals eager to be reached
This fortress is so rarely breached
The heart gives way as does the mind
And to this place are most men blind

The heart may beat, the soul is dead
Few put this thought into their head
For most men live between the lines
Refusing beasts and the divine

I am no different from all men
As stone my heart shaped by fate's winds
Abandoned hope and fled from grace
Until she crept into that space

Safe passage found she deep within
A bright white realm encased in sin
I desperate wicked, beyond cure
Her unearned love so clean, so pure

She pierced the soul of this man

His frail heart could barely stand

To take her in, admit I'm weak

Toward her soul now must I seek

Horse to water

You can lead this horse to water, but you will not
  make him drink

You can tell him that he's hasty, but he will not stop
  to think

You can ask him to be gentle, you can try to make
  him kind

If you want this man to love you, then you must let
  him unwind

You need to love everything, even those parts that
  make you cringe

If you try to make things perfect, then you're better
  off as friends

You need to take it all in stride and never force him
  to the well

If you need to knock the door down, then the other
  side is hell

You can scale the highest mountain, you can trove
  the deepest cave

You may preach the gospel loudly, but you cannot
  one soul save

You might find the hidden answer that's eluded all
  the wise

If you want this man to love you, then you'd better
  realize

You need to love everything, even those parts that make you seethe

It must survive the infancy and cut the baby teeth

You need to open up your heart and bear this constantly in mind

That to make a better man of me is going to take some time

You can run the longest race and make him suffer every mile

You may think his haste makes waste, although he needs it once in a while

You should hurry up and listen if you want to pass this test

If you want this man to love you, then don't expect from him the best

You need to love everything, even those parts that make you fear

It's irony, but set him free to make him hold you dear

You understand that hand in hand is not the only way

If your altar doesn't falter, then to the wrong God you pray

Contrast

Contrast, the virtuous gift of nature

By which we comprehend light from darkness

And all delights and dreads afforded the flesh

For who would know a deed born of charity

Without knowledge of those sewn in malice?

How could we cry tears of mourning

Without having the same burst forth from joy?

The cold, thin air of great heights appreciated

In the suffocating breaths of a summer's bog

Contrast, the tutor of kings and commons

All senses of men draw from her well of learning

We can delight in the nourishment of feast

For we have known pangs of fierce hunger

We afford those who weep true comfort

When we have experienced their pure rejoicing

True, therefore, by observation of this nature

That those who are forgiven little love little

This can only be known by the contrast

Of vicious, cruel men who in their hate

Magnify the glory of Judah's merciful Lion

Who by right and authority could justly condemn

By contrast, freely shines the light of His grace upon
the fallen

An everlasting contrast to the night shade of a man's
many sins

Indeed, for all these a season

And in seasons we likewise find contrast

She is the mystique of the human experience

For not all men may enjoy the starkness

Of her majesty

For those blessed to behold her raiments

Of vivid scarlet, deep purple and gold

They can live freely, with the fortitude granted

As contrast's greatest gift to man: humility

Got into life

Got into life, into life
Got in deep behind the veil
In a rush, in a hurry
Never tempted what I feared
Tempted what I feared

Let it bleed, let it bleed
Iron blood into my being
Didn't feel, tried to steal
An assassin at my heels
Assassin at my heels

There is nothing to be said
For what's been let into my head
Like communing with the dead
It has burrowed and brought out
What I dread

And it's creeping and seeping and weeping inside
I'm confused and abused as the little boy dies
Life comes down, it comes down to pain

Now I know, now I know

That the past has passed surreal

In a state, out of sorts

Pushing back and grinding all my gears

Grinding all my gears

I am running out of time

Expression captive to a rhyme

Sitting here waiting for a sign

Dreams strung up and hanging

From a vine

And it's creeping and seeping and weeping inside

I'm confused and abused as the little boy dies

Life comes down, it comes down to pain

Malice

Liars spinning, choke me
From their webbed lips poison drips

Fiends probe, provoke me
Use their sharp teeth to strip belief

Make me a newborn painting
Acquaint me
To a new way of thinking
Strip the canvas clean
Is sorrow or joy the dream?

Fools concoct, invoke me
Pour their malice into golden chalice

Villains rob, revoke me
Their fantasy, let innocence bleed

Make me a newfound island
A child again
Full of love and compassion
Be a spotless mind
Repeat it time after time

Lost world

Hello my friend, we meet again
You are my end and my first sin
I try no more to hide from fate
I so deplore this hopeless state

My life I've lived, my life I've slain
The more I've lived, the more I've pained
I have dismissed the love inside
Life heartless is all I've tried

Within my youth, I had been robbed
I cut my tooth on death and God
A child of lust, a child of need
A child who must have his good deed

I offer not, I offer all
But all is rot within these walls
I may descend into the bleak
I won't defend, for it is weak

Underwater

Underwater yet unnerved

Drowning is what I deserve

Would I, could I, change this fate?

In the deep and at death's gate

This the song that I have heard

Drowning is what I deserve

Will this tension inflict stress?

At my worst, another's best

I cannot repent with cause

Nor do I expect applause

Back and forth but so assured

Drowning is what I deserve

I could struggle to and fro

Life is but one long death throe

When one asks for answers true

Watch the masses come unglued

Walking upright yet interred

Drowning is what I deserve

A ride

One day I wandered out to ride
To find a place where I could hide
I drove into a quaint old town
But there was nobody around

The homes were classic and well-kept
With potted flowers lining steps
The front doors open as to greet
A neighbor's call to families meet

Yet no souls decked the open halls
A whitewashed tour of ghosted stalls
With windows down, I drove around
Until I heard a faint sweet sound

I drove a short way when I saw
A church to which the town was drawn
The bells were ringing high above
A choir within sang hymns of love

There were no cars in the small lot
I pulled into the closest spot
And took a step outside my car
Toward church doors slightly ajar

Approached I slowly to the doors
My heart was racing all the more
A chorus of voices within rang
The sparrow song is what they sang

And as I pressed upon the crack
A little sound took me aback
I quickly turned and with surprise
There stood a girl with bright blue eyes

Her hair was golden, long and straight
She looked no more the age of eight
She wore a yellow summer dress
Her snowy skin with no distress

She looked up with a bright young smile
I stood in awe for quite a while
Found not I how to ask her name
Perplexed was I by this small dame

She told me that her name was Faith
And when she spoke, I felt her grace
Then from her soft and wispy voice
She asked me had I made my choice

She studied me for my reply

A choice, what choice, did she imply?

Yet knew I not to ask her what

I felt she sensed within my gut

I reasoned not to lead her false

She like an angel, not to cross

Yet knew I what this question meant

For in my youth, my faith was spent

I told her yes, I'd made a choice

And this was not cause to rejoice

I told her to me church was dead

The word of God still in my head

And as I spoke, the world did fade

The little girl had gone away

And in her place, there stood a man

An ancient sage with dry cracked hands

His eyes all white were clearly blind

A face to whom time was unkind

His open hands contained a scroll

I took it and slowly unrolled

There was but one word on the page
I knew it well, it was my wage
For what I earned, it held within
My death was paid for by my sin

And sin the word so clearly inked
In red it stood, I could not blink
Then woke I from this dream in sweat
Its meaning painted my regret

The empty town, it was my heart
Idyllic world I did depart
The church abandoned long ago
Still watched my life through the sparrow

Faith from me by air was taken
The purest part of me forsaken
Her strength within her weakness lay
Oh, how her love did I betray

For in my driver's seat, I fled
This little town from which I sped
I left her there for I was sure
I'd have no pressing need of her

A fool is bound by useless thought

In worlds of wealth, we need Faith not

But take my learning and its breadth

The wages of our sin are death

Dark of night

Driving into dark of night
Storm clouds spreading frightful light
Each passing mile farther from home
Destination, me alone

Crashing drops of rain abound
In a sea of doubt, I drowned
Thinking I could work the maze
Kept me bound within life's cage

Dark recesses where I live
I forget, so I forgive
Thunderstorms, once they are past
How much longer will they last?

Dwellings in this confined space
No time to rest, no time to race
Sweet concoctions bide me time
Distractions framed in a rhyme

Crying past the midnight hour
Washed out road and broken mirror
Eternal sleep borne upside down
The bell has rung, the time is now

In mine

Tune into a station
That I've heard so oft before
So much contemplation proves
The wealthy life's a chore

That thing that I just thought
Is the most profound thus far
But of course, I did not capture it
The lid tight on the jar

Everybody wants something
That they themselves do not possess
Searching endlessly in circles
While this simple truth suppressed

There is no hope in living
When one life is there to live
And there's no point to redemption
When there's nothing to forgive

I suppose that the point of it
Is pointless at its best
To explore our every whim and thought
A gradeless, endless test

When I die

Living life in a state of sin
Left nothing out, let no one in
Kept the heart sterile
Let flesh go feral

A soul needs love to make amends
As sunset once far-off descends
I asked for mercy
While I lived earthly

The night I die, be by my side
My final thoughts I'll in you hide
The night I die, please hold my hand
That I might with the angels stand

Friends don't waver when the earth shakes
In hard times lovers don't forsake
Watch the river rise
Above mountainside

Riddles, questions, endless quarrels
Can peace grow absent of morals?
Starlight needs the void
Proving out our joy

The night I die, be by my side

My final thoughts I'll in you hide

The night I die, please hold my hand

That I might with the angels stand

The great matter

It is a great matter of conscience

To rightly divide the word of truth

Upon the thin blade of mortal valuations

Do we offer our souls to the heavens?

For the pointed edge of wit and merit

May delude those who by dark hours

Wallow in the self-knowledge of doubt

And pitiable as they may be when unseen

Cast no shade of question to those

Who by their radiant speeches derive

Their sole confidence and purpose

Nay, truth does not whither under suppressing

Flames of the malcontent's retributive lusts

Truth, steadfast in its sublime reality

Is as constant as the decay of time

Is as royal as a king's jeweled crown

Is as pure as a mother's love

Is as strong as an unmerited sacrifice

Is as eternal as the one by whose hand

All truth is dispersed across creation

Chapter 2: Pain

What is a man?

What is a man
Whose heart turned stone?
Once gentle, young
Grows old alone
What is a man
Whose name is lost?
Defends his state
But at what cost?

I am a man
Becoming sore
Afraid of that
Which most ignore
I am a man
Whose days run thin
Repenting to
Make room for sin

What is a man
Whose eyes can't see
In front of him
The other's need?

What is a man

Whose words don't bind?

Will not commit

Just redefine

I am a man

Who inward seeks

The verses where

Our dreams do speak

I am a man

Who hesitates

And this is why

I'll not be great

Victor May

Victor May was once a man
Once a man indeed
And as men know, as all men grow
They seek their destiny

Victor May was raised up poor
And from rank poverty
When success comes, this one thing
All friends become more greed

Victor May did marry young
She was true beauty
Yet Victor grew to see the void
Of life's disparity

Victor May set forth alone
To find a name for he
Abandoning a faith in grace
For devil's certainty

Victor May opened a door
Whence no soul may return
The other side, another world
Where light will not endure

Victor May became a thing
A beast of dark design
Unleashed he here upon the earth
Apocalyptic signs

Victor May subdued the earth
Mastering his slaves
Brutality cannot deter
As righteous men still pray

Victor May considered not
The power of spilt blood
When faithful bleed and thus are freed
Cannot repel the flood

Victor May fell by five words
Those he most reviled
This poison came through by his ears
"You are your father's child"

Trapped

The room was white

Down long halls grey

My hands were bound

Along the way

I did not know

Why I was there

I did not know

I did not care

Two black suits

On either side

Two stone faces

Four cold eyes

The room was bright

The room was grim

Was it for me

Or just for them?

They did not speak

I did not move

Their silent gazes

Set the mood

I was cold

The shackles, lead

They scrubbed me raw

And shaved my head

What had happened?

What transpired?

What had I done

To draw such ire?

The silence lingered

For a spell

For how long

I could not tell

But then one spoke

To ask my name

The question scratched

Against my brain

I did not know

Just who I was

Or how I got

To where I was

Their eyes exchanged

A subtle glance

They narrowed as

My mind went black

They asked again

What was my name

I blankly stared and

Just the same

I welcomed answers

More than they

The room was white

The long halls grey

Then he snapped

He snapped my mind

My eyes rolled back

I was not mine

My skin it crawled

The men flew back

On the floor sprawled

My muscles burst

The chains they broke

The air rushed out

The two men choked

My body quaked

Room upended

Blew out the door

Time suspended

Many voices

Filled up the halls

I felt like I

Stood ten feet tall

I walked myself

Into the fray

A dozen men

With guns did spray

The slugs, they struck

The slugs, they stung

I felt my blood

Begin to run

But all the smoke

And acrid air

Could not subdue

The beast they feared

I saw myself

Run through grey halls

I saw the men

Be rent and fall

I made it out

Of the dark maze

The building tall

The sirens blazed

To the forest

Through barbed fence

I sprinted fast

I didn't wince

It was freezing

There was snow

I was lost

Nowhere to go

My eyes saw clear

As deer they fled

The trail behind

Me covered red

My breath ran short

My body shook

I fell to ground

My blood ran thick

The winter's air

Became so cold

I was yet young

But felt so old

What had I been

Moments before

I felt true death

Knock at my door?

I was a man

I was a beast

I was a man

Caught in between

A life to live

A life to take

My body sprawled

On frozen lake

Of ice, where snow

Stretched out like ash

And there beyond

I saw my past

Dancing ghostly

Through the fog

At one time I

Had been a god

Or something close

Yes, something near

And now my skin

Felt cold, felt fear

I was alone

Upon this lake

I was alone

My choice to make

And as the blood

Filled in my eyes

In its warmth

I realized

My sacrifice

To long cheat death

Required I

Take many breaths

Away from those

Purer than I

Away from those

High in the skies

From where they sit

I will be judged

My soul singed black

By this my grudge

That I could not

Attain the goal

My father's glory

Not my own

There I prayed

Desperately

One last hope for

Amnesty

I took my place

Amongst the trees

A resting place

For my disease

And be so warned

By this my tale

Hate heals no wound

Greed always fails

And if you are

To be set free

Forgiveness unlocks

Divinity

It's what we need

More than our lives

Forgiveness is

True sacrifice

From where I sit

From where I stand

I see right through you

What you want

And all you do

You see me as I see you see

What we are and who we will be

From where I sit

I see the world turn

What it wants

All the lives it burns

It makes me, makes me, its master

Life goes fast, death comes much faster

From where I think

I see inside me

Is my mind

The one thing not free?

I lose sleep, no sleep, one nightmare

Struggle to find one hope, one care

Put to rest

Stuck between the dead of night

Shall I sleep, oh sleepless fright

Dreams insist I mind awake

Nightmares do I so self-create

Visions of joy out of sync

Dreams of hopes flushed down the sink

Is this life, life to be lived?

All my wonders have been sieved

Through a filter etched in pain

Fixed in a whitewashed tomb of stains

Accept I this before my sleep

That this night of pitch black deep

Consume my mind, steal my soul

And wander aimless for a goal

That sneaks away upon the search

My will and effort upon scorched earth

So beset my eyes on gold

To no other my story told

Until the day of my last breath

This cancer finally put to rest

Night of dream

The first crash came before we woke

The second came, and no one spoke

The house it rocked

The house it swayed

Our little family fell and prayed

The children ran into the room

The children frightened by the boom

Sounds I had not heard before

Sounds of which blew out the doors

Voices whispered in the wind

Whispering for us our sins

I knew this voice, I knew so well

I heard this voice drag me to hell

Conversations of the past

Conversations made of glass

None to which to prick the soul

None to reach perfection's goal

Here upon the altar spread

Here all worried thought and dread

Spoke my children for their lives

Spoke I comfort, wretched lies!

All forsaken, all for not

All my fruitful works were rot

And the storm consumed the home

And wished I had been unknown

Proof to be heard or be seen

Proof that offerings unclean

Now the turbulence of air

Now the vanity of prayer

Turned and twisted by the force

Turned to ash by the due course

Of the time and of the hour

Of the loss of mortal power

May we be saved from the storm

May my children know not this harm!

Woke then I from dreadful vision

Woke I now, know not division

Might be this my wakeup call

Might I reason not to fall

Into the trap of little lies

Into the vast pit which belies

Those reigned realities

Those trifled trivialities

Let me rise above the fray

Let me live just one more day

For I swear to break the mold

For I swear my children's souls!

I will make myself to truth

I will lead us out of this room

Blunt nature

Mountain strong, rooted deep in earth

Sculpted by epochs undated

Immovable, resolute will

Rescue my lost soul!

Could this darkness within be crushed?

I would ask thee, oh great stone,

Rise up and fall upon me

Under thy innumerable mass may I find peace

For I am bound by a dark prince

Whose ruby-adorned opal crown

Bares scaly, dense, impenetrable armor

Unblinking, cruel eyes consumed with hellfire

Thick scarlet veins pumping blood of saints

Dislocated by fear, I fall before my master

What hope and joy, nurtured by innocence

Painfully wrest from bruised fists

Jagged nails burrow into sweating flesh

Channels of my palms flow with blood

As my last bastion of resistance gives way

Oh pitiful soul!

What creature have you granted safe passage

Across those regions set aside for grace?

My vessel a plaything for sleepless evil

The caregiver of guilt and repentance hath
abandoned me

Silver shield of conscience melted

By heat of passion and fulfilled desire

The green vine of kindness

Once growing wildly and freely

Around a child's springtime dreams

Become a constricting serpent

Coiled tightly 'round this heart of ash

Venomous fangs embedded in his prize

Poison of unrepentant lies pump

Across the synapses of my mind

Implanting detestable visions of deplorable deeds

Breaths become faint as

My illusion of humanity, necrotic

Toxic blood makes necrotic

My unsullied humanity

Wars and worlds

Wars and worlds are made of men
Each conspire, yet neither win
Similarly bound to sin
Wars and worlds are made of men

Skies and shields are made to save
Protecting clever and the knave
Stalling swordplay and the grave
Skies and shields are made to save

Beast and rose are twins at heart
In either maw one torn apart
Inert until the hunger starts
Beast and rose are twins at heart

I didn't ask

Little infections crawl under my skin
Letting out creatures I didn't let in
Every reddened pock, hardened new scar
Ask me one question, prove that I'm a liar

I didn't ask for what I have
Excess is a venomous staff
Poisons good intention's path
I didn't ask for what I have

Waning retention, sordid memories
Infecting love with lust, the poet's disease
Parents try their best, often make the worst
But it's not their fault, all of us are cursed

I didn't ask for what I have
Excess is a venomous staff
Poisons good intention's path
I didn't ask for what I have

I want, I want

I want strong

But I love weakness

Watch as I turn brightness

Bleakness

I do not love

What does love me

I do not want it

If it's free

I want grit

But have no patience

To pain I am never

Gracious

I do not seek

What does seek me

I am misled by

Simple things

I want hope

But have no reason

All my faith is somehow

Treason

I do not pray

Although I should

Perhaps in truth

I never could

I never could

The End of Us

Today I got the call I dread
I knew her words as they were said
What we were, now to her dead
My heart sank to my feet like lead

What had I done to make this end?
What other message could I send?
This promise I still not rescind
That I would always be her friend

The end of us, my heart in flames
The end of us, can't stand this pain
The end of us, still I can't blame
The end of us, I'll never be the same

Tomorrow I see nothing new
Nothing but visions of you
How can a good thing turn so cruel?
I have no hope to see me through

What could I've done to make it right?
She filled my dreams and made them bright
She was my sky, my starry night
For her, my life a sacrifice

The end of us, my heart in flames

The end of us can't, stand this pain

The end of us, still I can't blame

The end of us, I'll never be the same

Tested

A wanderer through school, outlying

Anxiety pouring and controlling

Wishing for another shell

Restless sleep, headphones save me

I wasn't loved or liked

Didn't make the team

Reading up at night

Wished it was a dream

Tested, at a young age bested

Tossed into a storm

Never protected

Punishment, shame and pain

Traveling companions

Tested, at a young age bested

Never found a job satisfying

Impatience, impertinence, destroying

Tried so many different things

None my own and none my face

I wasn't esteemed

Didn't make the cut

Opportunity

Just another rut

Tested, at adult age bested

Tossed into a storm

Never protected

Punishment, shame and pain

Traveling companions

Tested, at adult age bested

What comes next?

We know it never ceases

Each adventure one of my diseases

And by long years, tested

And by long years, tested

Come down

Come down and reach me
Reach for me grasping
This sad soul is breaking apart
Down in the shadows
Shadows of greatness
Far past the red line I've crossed

Come down and join me
Join me, start falling
You'll never know light till it's dark
Caught in the vacuum
The vacuous fortune
Where our ideals are stalled

Oh, such a pitiful bounty
Is this the sum, all I've wrought?
One glance to see I'm lonely
Never understood, I refused to be taught
Now nothing's all I've got

Come down and take me
Take me for granted

Make my mind starve for the start

Go forth and lay claim

Claim the uncharted

Make me go win back your heart

Oh, such a pitiful bounty

Is this the sum, all I've wrought?

One glance to see I'm lonely

Never understood, I refused to be taught

Now nothing's all I've got

Suffer me

Take my voice, make it still
Another lonely discourse
Brisk rebuke, lingering quill
Restless, endless remorse

Suffer me, suffer you
Suffering is what we do
Release me, release you
Freedom, the hardest to choose

Patient merit, unworthy takes
Lamenting choices guessed
Gospel rot, true love forsakes
Once confident, distressed

Suffer me, suffer you
Suffering is what we do
Release me, release you
Freedom, the hardest to choose

Never wanted, so received
Prayers unrequited
Abrogate and so deceived
Immolate, enlighten

Suffer me, suffer you

Suffering is what we do

Release me, release you

Freedom, the hardest to choose

My friend across the country rests

It's late, it's cold, why am I writing?

Because my heart and mind are fighting

My friend across the country rests

Cancer swarms beneath his chest

A world away, two worlds apart

He broke my will, I broke his heart

My friend across the country rests

I am but conceited flesh

I want, I wish, to make him well

But if he were, I'd never tell

My friend across the country rests

He turned my weakness to prowess

We oft repel what brings us joy

A trick our devils oft deploy

My friend across the country rests

I'll shepherd his soul's confidence

Enemy in shadow

Shadowy night, creeping upon me

I lie paralyzed

Figure, serpentine but movement jagged

It approaches from long dim hall

Eyes cast deep yellow beams of terror

I am seized

Each breath a focused struggle

Escaping existence, the kindest dream

But the nightmare yet approaches

Rapping of sharp claws on aged wood

I scream silently

Nails of glass crack and shriek along the walls

Prayers fast and furious spent

Seal these crystal tears to my lead pillow

I beg forgiveness

Some deed done has summoned this thing

Bringing with it the weeping and gnashing

Odorless smoke billows from its spiraled horns

Death, upon a midnight making

I seek comfort

Absent nostrils, thin wiry mouth in frozen grin

No mind has concocted such a beast

Flesh electric stands on edge as it studies

I force consciousness

Latching onto some element of reality

There must be a bridge to lucidity

And yet it consumes me, what have I become?

What is right

What is right, not always clear
Sometimes it's what we hold dear
Thus, it shifts like wandering sands
Acceptance is what we withstand

What is right, it can depend
When tasked we like hot metal bend
Glowing red our aspirations
Living in a zombie nation

What is right, derived by faith
The righteous echo history's greats
Men of season protest loudly
Pronouns wicked, say they proudly

What is right, may stand out plainly
Yet to say so, say so insanely
Humankind banishes His truth
That's why we all accept his ruse

Precious light

Light so precious
As ships descend
Drift to blackness
Upon their end

Deep in the sea
No ode reprieves
The masters sleep
None remain to grieve

What signpost there
To mark the way?
What terrors lurk
In murky waves?

Light so precious
As winters freeze
Wages of sin
Reality

Abandon hope
Bring forth the pain
Repent and turn
Blot out the stain

Crouch and cower

Come enemy

Prove I am

Infinity

Leap stone

Been trying to forget

Why, I can't remember

Maybe living with regret

Makes July feel like December

Going to need another day

To let another year get past

Don't see another way

Guess I'm just going to outlast

Leap stone, butterfly

In a world of constant aching

Need to leap by

Leap stone, let it fly

Getting warmer by the shaking

Need to leap by

The harder the rains fall

The less I can forget her

Go up so fast I stall

Below me is the winter

I'll ask another time

Is it time to write the letter?

I am punished, so I rhyme

Hope has left me cold and bitter

Leap stone, butterfly

In a world of constant aching

Need to leap by

Leap stone, let it fly

Getting warmer by the shaking

Need to leap by

Silhouette

Shadows come to life before my eyes

Slender creatures evading the light

Lust of dreams and visions violate

Substance each of us create

Silhouette

Outlines vying for my mind

Visions space and time cannot define

Shaded by lost moments and regret

Living there, within my silhouette

Humor is the wormwood of my soul

Parasites prevent from me my goal

Ends and means don't justify the way

Listen to what darkness has to say

Silhouette

Outlines vying for my mind

Visions space and time cannot define

Shaded by lost moments and regret

Living there, within my silhouette

Broken wings and flame soar into night

Shadows wax and wane by candlelight

Seek out faith while my will surrenders

Where is my silhouette's defender?

Silhouette

Outlines vying for my mind

Visions space and time cannot define

Shaded by lost moments and regret

Living there, within my silhouette

Coming back for more

How much pain can a single soul endure?
Does the sickness satisfy you?
Or does the drama have allure?
When the snow melts in my heart
Is that the time your hope draws near?
If the summer never comes
Will it be more than you can bear?

Coming back, coming back
Coming back for more
Taking what you can get
But always wanting more

How many times can you balm the stinging wounds?
Will you ever seek another
To fill your midnight with new moons?
Can they mend your broken heart
With fresh passions unexplored?
You keep thinking you'll get back
What you pushed so far out the door

Coming back, coming back
Coming back for more
Taking what you can get
But always wanting more

Let me loose

I feel the hate within me
My dreams at night berate me
Accept this I insanely
Know I where I go

I sense conflict within me
My vainness veiled thinly
Denial I most certainly
Mastered oh so well

Let me loose, set me free
All I want to be is me
Let me loose, light my wire
Give me wings, lift me higher

I trust what I cannot see
Connecting blank points plainly
Maybe I'll get there safely
Let's not rule it out

I want love to live in me

To stimulate and save me

The problem is I can't be

That is why I sing

Let me loose, set me free

All I want to be is me

Let me loose, light my wire

Give me wings, lift me higher

Downward went the day

Downward went the day

That changed

Everything

Couldn't tell you why

It changed

Everything

Oh, how the day falls

From lofty midnight visions

And now, today it crashes

Downward went the day

So strange

Everything

Went a different way

So strange

Everything

Oh, how the day falls

Why tease me midnight visions

To leave today in ashes

I suck at what I do

I suck at what I do

I fail at what I try

I want to be like you

I won't because I'm shy

I suck at what I do

I lament what I know

I cannot see what's true

I dare not let it show

I suck at what I do

I wish that I did not

I will not let you through

I think such simple thoughts

I suck at what I do

I do not know the way

I act as if I knew

I have no more to say

Lungs

Suffocation is a most heinous of strategies

Starving lungs lap at the warm air leaking through cold, tight grip

Contracting in sharp, arrhythmic strains as they gasp vainly for survival

Crying out as exposed hatchlings to a song bird never to return

Bind the creature with barbed wire

Make his struggle intensely tortuous

Does the deep frost crack when exposed to a river of bondage?

Without the fresh air of creativity, the mind is but a vapid instrument

Pox descends upon constricted lungs

Blackening the native hue of inspiration

Fear of loss and betrayal

Toxins that poison hope and encouragement

Muted repercussions from distant sins pollute one's atmosphere

Unclean air mocks lungs as saltwater to relentless thirst

Mutagens invade, infesting healthy cells with disease

Searing, cancerous lesions

Lungs give out under this terrible mass and die unknown, unknowing

Wealthy

Behold, the wealthy rise
Above the city, to the skies
Built by lowly hands, despised
On poverty's back the wealthy rise

Hallmarks of their vanity
Disdain for humanity
Incessant greed, rapacity
Incestuous their vanity

Behold, the gluttonous roar
Gems they more than men adore
What does fate have for them in store?
We rummage while they roar

Bulwarks steel with ornate bars
Within them plenty, without them starve
Their acts from hell, they claim the stars
Protected there behind their bars

Behold, their excess waste
Waves of suffering in their wake
Ascending on the backs they break
Leaving us to clean their waste

I hate the stars

I hate the stars

For all they are

Reminding us that God is far

A trillion little nighttime scars

They cut the mind like glassy shards

I hate the stars

For all they are

Only eons do they spar

Outliving all us mortal jars

Patronizing all our wars

Infernal bulbs, eternal spots

A thousand worlds before one drops

And finally when they reach death's gate

They leave a void no light escapes

I hate the stars

For all they are

Breaking hearts and filling bars

Countless they, though spread afar

Congest the sky like crowded cars

I hate the stars

For all they are

Reaping madness like satyrs

The near without protection chars

Spreading cancer to all that are

Infernal bulbs, eternal spots

A thousand worlds before one drops

And finally when they reach death's gate

They leave a void no light escapes

I don't want

I don't want to be everything
I don't want to be anything
I'm better off being on my own
I'm better off singing my own song

I don't need to impress
But I always seem to repress
The part of me that makes me, me
The solace in insanity

I don't need an idea to instill
I don't need telling how to feel
If the world abandons me, I'm fine
Here or there, it's only time

I care not for the cares of men
I know my will, I share their sin
Everyone is in it for themselves
Everyone is warding off their hell

I won't be hostage to these fears I
won't satisfy you with my tears
Let me burn, I'm happy in a cell
If I don't yearn, I'm miserable as well

I don't have many things to say
It really doesn't matter anyway
What I have is not for you to take
What I am is not something you could make

I'm not angry or impressed
I'm not upset or depressed
I just want to walk this lonely road
I like it when my inner star implodes

End game

Standing on a tower at noon
Looking down on the monsoon
Seems a good day to take a dive
And for a moment, feel alive

Nothing purposed ever seen
Not like on the silver screen
The scripted hopes and weary scenes
Blackened fields of broken dreams

Summer's sun is burning down
Beads of sweat worn like a gown
End game achieved finally
The next move is not to be

Nothing purposed ever seen
Not like on the silver screen
The scripted hopes and weary scenes
Blackened fields of broken dreams

Man's last step like eagle's first
Within a flash, the spirit bursts
Out of madness comes such violence
But all that sought was just the silence

My heart

Its genesis fear, selfishness clear
It had gone around, guilty party found

My heart, my heart, slowly breaking down
Each beat so painful, in my chest it pounds

With a shock it came, sudden intense pain
Woke me from a dream, made me want to scream

My heart, my heart, into the abyss
The rhythm is lost, so many beats missed

Rest was not to be, my God set me free
Salvation rejoice, damnation my choice

My heart, my heart, why did I betray?
Draining my life force, time for me to pay

Rob me

You rob me of my confidence
Questioning my common sense
Levy judgment on my guilt
Tilted towers have I built

You cared not for the hope I had
Left to search as a nomad
Wandering deserts in my head
A weighted soul envies the dead

You stole from me my virgin dreams
Pool of visions no more teem
Demand you still the best I have
Now it's pain to even laugh

You turned this boy into a wretch
What illness did you let me catch?
Dark spaces are now all I find
Trapped within my sullied mind

Grant me this, O Lord

Grant me this, O Lord, a peaceful rest
From which this troubled mind not wake
Let the many sins of my flesh wither
With these soluble bones
Fear I not the shore across the sea
But only her means of passage

Grant me this, O Lord, before my reckoning
To love purely, absent self-devotion and need
Let my actions be as resolute as my word
Which flow effortlessly from the mind's tongue
My inward voice, sewn in my mother's womb
Cries out for the redemption of sacrifice
Affirm these hands and free my spirit

Grant me this, O Lord, a quietus calm
Released evermore of temporal pangs
Let them flutter away on sparrows' wings
The daggers of unreciprocated affection
Overwhelm the most steadfast of hearts
Steady, therefore, these hands
May their strike be swift and true

Fire cry

Tonight, I saw a fire cry
Glowing ash of broken pride
Unfulfilled but not denied
Tonight, I saw a fire cry

Tonight, I saw a fire cry
And thus, I must soliloquize
Pain, my nerves have cauterized
Tonight, I saw a fire cry

Tonight, I saw a fire cry
Flowing embers, wild eyes
By death alone we canonize
Tonight, I saw a fire cry

Tonight, I saw a fire cry
Loss is love, I've realized
Shipwrecked is my paradise
Tonight, I saw a fire cry

My last word

My God, my heart has turned to stone
Wade I through the mass alone
Forsaken I, and all my faith
Torn apart by aimless grace

My mom, my love has gone so cold
I age, but this pain won't grow old
Forgive me, and what I do
I only want blessings for you

My son, my mind cannot see right
For you, my son, I've tried to fight
Yet this break cannot be mended
Live life as I'd not existed

My daughter, you are a bright star
Where I go is where you are
Wait there I until your date
Embrace your time for you are great

My wife, you sit above them all
My hopeless soul is not your fault
I wish I had not done you harm
Snared I was by devil's charm

My love, you are the one last thing
The reason why these tears now stream
I fought for you, succumbed to death
Your eyes the life of my last breath

Chapter 3: Love

Silence

Silence, sipping madly on inspiration
Capturing the chorus, perspiration
Be thoughtful, my salutation
Sharing her power of sensation

My phoenix, flaming firmament
This love certain, permanent
Her eyes, bright, resplendent
Graceful as her temperament

Gray skies pass thee haplessly
Born ye stars, endlessly
Painting them all carefully
Sweat for you, ceaselessly!

Her virtue drives me extolling
Cry out these verses, controlling
Defining virtue, patrolling
Desire for her lips, scalding

Thunder, cascading listlessly
Seize her essence, divinity
Inching close, reality
Brave together, infinity!

Across the table

Across an empty table
Staring back at me
Goblet full of promises
Shake the shade of suspicion
Reach out and hold her
Lay claim before she claims leave

Inside, the flood returns
Droplets they once were
Born within the dust of doubt
Come now, let the right one in
Here, her hand outstretched
Patiently for her partner

Passion, deep bass in the heart
Thudding nerves, pulsing
Electric resurrection
Tapping into a dense well
Flow many waters
Be the tide on her new shore

Prose, unfolding as a rose

Red lips beckoning

Method certainly madness

Release the apprehension

Embrace, warmth resounds

Melodiously, we're moved

Would she accept, one more verse?

Two souls connected

By true profundity, love

She is ancient, she is new

Our sea, adventure

We, together forever!

Sojourn

One empty glass into a sojourn

Little time for these feeble hands

To capture those things unsearchable

Unknowable, as history portends

Start up again and let it flow

Don't stall for perfection

If you can write it, capture it

Try, and in so doing, free thyself

Mix the burden with pleasure

Let not the mind be ruled by the schemes

That others would have you become

Everyone needs a program

To make it through a performance

Unconsummated perfection

Thus, the struggle continues

And we find that we are more apt to seek

Than to simply accept what has been found

But in those quiet moments

Within the rhythm of another's melody

We find our voicing

And then, we sing, we sing!

Be heard, soft voices

Be heard, timid souls

Thy name is glory and thy purpose, profound!

Repeat and repeat and hear the new sound

Would you let this new seed take root?

Roots, connected and buried deep within soft earth

Storms, chased away by winds of change

Roots, roots are strong if they are bound

To the other's thirst and need for light

Give room to each for maturity

Give space to each for absorption of truth

In our subtle space can a mark be made

Permanent, powerful

We would have not known this reality

Had we not given ourselves up to fortune

Not to the peculiarity of those random events

Which are unshapely and void of purpose

No, we are seen through the looking glass

Accepting a script resolves us unencumbered

Therefore, a choice is itself, purpose

And this, I know in the parts of me I do not know

I love a creature of bright flame!

Her heat, protective, a shield for this man of wax

Quickly, capture this kindling within me

Strike a match from her smile

And illuminate the dark spaces within me

Realize forgiveness is her hand

Mercy is her eyes

Salvation, her hand in mine

I love her

I will cherish her

I will, by devotion, consume her heart

And she will save mine

Phoenix burn

Across the world or just the bar

In fact, no matter where you are

Smile and take the time to realize

Just how lovely life is at times

There are old, and there are young

In between the total sum

Of what we are, or we could be

In fact, let's claim nobility

Why not? Others have without a cause

It would be nice to sometimes pause

But that's for later, not for now

Now we're here, and we know how

That the way a good sign goes

It fits so nicely with sound prose

That's why we take the time to think

Or perhaps fill a third time drink

Aren't you glad it's where we've come?

Aren't you glad we're always young?

Just look around, look think see

What then this resistivity!?

Let it go and let it in

Make a joy filled decision

Laden, latent conversations

Truth the most restful station

For you to speak, for us to learn

And so, my Phoenix, burn, burn, burn

Thanks, again

I do not thank you quite enough
For all your many gifts
I take for granted that you're tough
Assumptions make me drift

But here I sit, thinking through
All those joys you bring
Every day I age I'm new
On those days you sing!

Yes, I wrestle with my past
Grappling broken dreams
Your smile shouts, "We will outlast!"
Let's walk the balance beam

That is life, worn to its core
A pit of snags, snakes, snares
For this I'm thankful most of all
My struggle thou hast shared

Pen

Some say I pen with mighty gift
Some may regard this useless script
Yet I can beg integrity
My pen reflects humanity!

I do not wish to reap squalor
Still I push to sit and ponder
What things we cannot define
Yes, I point to the divine!

How else could I change mind's eye
Devious and deep inside?
Great storms born of happenstance?
I see will in their advance!

Drink some till no longer merry
I prefer my mind stay airy
Let us reach and touch the void
Pray no converse we avoid

Contesting I, against these odds
Pitied heavens and their gods
For what sits across from me
The best thing that I'll ever see

Simple words

If I wrote you simple words
Then would my true love be heard?
I am not gifted in voice
Not a strong man, not by choice
What then can I offer you?
What then can I offer you?

All I have and all I'll be
Every dream that I can see
All my grace and charity
Every possibility

If I cast you a sincere gaze
Would you return to this maze?
The path forward oft is gray
I'll be by you every day
What then can I offer you?
What then can I offer you?

All the wealth these bones can bear
Every scar and all their prayers
All my fear and childhood tears
As you make them disappear

I've decided

I've decided that I'm proud of you
I pass a glance, you see it through
You make the crops grow after rain
And harvest purpose as the grain

I've decided that I'll follow you
I go off course, while you keep true
You are a window without stain
Stars by night and sun by day

I've decided that I'll worship you
I muddy waters you keep blue
You refine hope from earthy vain
And thread shared sorrows to our name

I've decided that I'll honor you
Blood and bruises prove virtue
We are the pair who were ordained
To claim our world and be reclaimed

Bright night

Look up into this bright, bright night

The air is cool and all alright

Do you see the same as me?

Me with you and you with me

Vocabulary, often slacking

You make me make you make me proud

I'm going to be clear now

Joy is fulfillment of a need

Take a good look at my stare

In every burden, take my care

I am your friend, but am I yours?

Nothing's certain, my love sure

Tributaries, often lacking

You make me make you sing aloud

From countless faces in a crowd

Yours, the only one I need

Suppose

Suppose I try another time
Romancing is utterly sublime
My second go still for your hand
Every other promise sand
Love me as I love you true
Let me love you, see troubles through

Suppose you try another time
To clean a soul and make it shine
Your efforts have not gone for naught
You've brought rains to an endless drought
Your love will return to you
Let my reflection be that truth

Suppose we try another time
To help each other be refined
Our partnership a watershed
One moment for one lifetime fed
In wilderness we heard the call
We will not let the other fall

Fight hard

Every time you stumble, you crumble

Feel like giving up

Once again, diving in, think it's easy

Then realize that you're growing up

Nothing comes, nothing sums

Like the dreams you know you've left behind

Assassinate, complicate

What is plain can be so hard to sustain

Fight hard, fight hard for the ones you love

You think you say, said you say it

You don't say it enough

The mystery was conceived long ago

And from far above

Fight hard, fight hard for the ones you love

No correction

Instill in me a sense of calm
Don't withdraw those loving arms
I'm so happy when you're near
So happy when you're near

Encourage me, I'll pass the test
In troubled days your nighttime rest
I'm so happy when you're here
So happy when you're here

There is no correction
You're my sworn protection
Endless satisfaction
There is no correction

Command me, point the way to go
Together, all ways lead us home
I'm so happy that it's clear
So happy that it's clear

There is no correction
Partners share but one direction
Truth through introspection
There is no correction

Rapid Response

Evenings, pleasures

Stored up treasures

All our merriment endeavors

Midnights, grasping

Wake up gasping

Passion that is everlasting

Hello, sweetness

Goodbye, sickness

Perfect pitch in joy and sadness

Whispers, rocking

Feel us talking

Underwater, in the heavens

Compress gently

Evidently

Time is up, it's time for resting

Let's get back to us

We've come a long, long way
A journey neither predicted
We've had the starts and stops
Acquainted and restricted

Yet here we are, still flying true
Bumpy streams may come
We blaze right on through
Together a greater sum

Let's get back to us
Wandering the road of trust
Struggles yes, levity too
Let's make the most of me and you

We've moved fast, advanced slowly
At times matching the pace of snails
Your trust in me not taken lightly
Let's be the dreams of fairy tales

We love, we fight, we make it right
You and I, an incredible team
Complementing, matching
We the eyes of love unseen

Let's get back to us

Wandering the road of trust

Struggles yes, levity too

Let's make the most of me and you

A simple song

Howdy there my muffin
You're sweet and warm and luvin
Blueberry and sugar
I rap because I love her!

Simple songs are the best
Better than the baffling rest
Give her words of sweet elevation
And watch the train glide into station

Hi, hi, hi and merry ho!
It's not Christmas but you glow
Like lights weaved through a snowy tree
You take, you make, the most of me!

You say hello and I say come in
You're better than any show binged
Compelling my mind to high places
Fixing smiles on all my faces

Simple songs are the best
Better than the baffling rest
Give her words of sweet elevation
And watch the train glide into station

Say to me, say to you

In silence we meet again

Negotiating each other's sins

What becomes of deadened trust?

We weep and blame and color

Promising to not betray the other

We have not known the best of us

Say to me

Say to you

Say it loud, say it true

We are, each other

Lie on me

Lie on you

Don't deny what we've been through

We are, each other

Troubles make their way to us

Retaliation somehow a must

Forgiveness, something we forgot

We have jumped, and we survived

Pleading the truth in the tears we've cried

Together we shape our future

Say to me

Say to you

Say it loud, say it true

We are, each other

Lie on me

Lie on you

Don't deny what we've been through

We are, each other

You and I

You say I am forgiven
But what that really means
You want my soul's confession
You want laid bare the truth

But what you have forgotten
Not all is what it seems
Why yield this one concession?
Why deliver the proof?

I rinse, repeat, and say it
Each strike the blade more blunt
I race slowly in circles
Evading stalking shame

But I try to remember
That love is not a haunt
For beasts and ghosts to savor
It comes back to the truth

Intricate

Intuition, subjugated
Innocence is complicated
Addled, riddled, trickled down
Lowly, slowly dripped to ground

Infiltrated, masqueraded
Intubated, inhalated
Little troubles slink and slither
Becoming great before they whither

I search her form, intoxicating
The way she moves, exhilarating
Her charm ceaseless, scintillating
Her eyes affection, intimidating

Incubated, separated
Introspection, segregated
Lustful, hopeful, drawn and quartered
Licking wounds of bled emotions

Intimated, suffocated

Injuries are celebrated

Saddled, whittled, sunk and drowned

Buried deep beneath the ground

I seek her soft love, penetrating

Immortalize her, consecrating

Her soul is gold, no debating

Magnetic cords compelled and craving

Emote

Don't drill holes in my emotions

You've never set sail on this ocean

You are first and I am last

Yet you're the one who gives up fast

Don't lie to me and make me bleed

You've dangled me with Damocles

You are quick and I am slow

Yet you don't know which way to go

I'm going to emote

Deal with it

I make you full

Don't forget

I'm going to emote

Make me full

Deal with the push and pull

Don't mock me for my pricking fears

You've said you cared and shared my tears

You are slick and I am stone

Yet you'd prefer to go alone

Don't set me up to make me fall

You've climbed up high and there you stall

You are cold and I am flame

Yet we make magic all the same

I'm going to emote

Deal with it

I make you full

Don't forget

I'm going to emote

Make me full

Deal with the push and pull

Black and white

Be to me my black and white

Separate the dark from light

Instill in me the will to fight

Love me for my black and white

Be to me my balanced scale

Make me strong where most are frail

Show me truth behind the veil

Love both sides, a balanced scale

Be to me my cold night's fire

Consume me with your heart's desire

Eternally I'll be inspired

Ignited by my cold night's fire

Be to me my black and white

Make me blind, give me my sight

Pure and strong, our bond is tight

For love we both our black and white

Where love begins

Sunshine eclipsed
By weathered skies
One journey starts, one journey dies
A sunset met by a sunrise
Ancient emotion realized

Waves of hope the tide brings in
Can good come from what we're told is sin?
Who can say how love begins?
What purpose served to hide within?

Upon the breeze there comes a song
Its melody makes short the long
Dividing time, and right from wrong
To whom, or what, the source belongs?

Unlike the bell, it tolls for few
Its Spartan touch makes old souls new
A currency one can't accrue
An act of faith to know it's true

The joy of some, the bane of some

When it draws near some stay, some run

None can say how it's begun

Our spirits are around it spun

This brings the story back to thee

As we set out on this journey

Can doubt and pain and death and greed

Be swallowed by this burning need?

And how to know if this is right?

It came like stranger in the night

Yet for this feeling I will fight

Let's make the mountains feel the might

Cool my head and heart as wind

I'll travel to earth's distant ends

Pursue this peace as war rescinds

I finally know where love begins

Inspired

Know this

I feel you

Radiating from my heart

Passion and fear

Throbbing

My organs twist and turn

Visions of us warm my mind

Unlock this frozen heart

So again, I dream

Blood pumping

Nerves on fire

Seeing you, holding you

Unlimited potential

Energy and clarity

Skip stones over tranquil waters

Of my soul

Be thou my vision

Return me to home

Toils and troubles they may be

Let this rain fall

To pass onward

From which we shall grow

And be one

Meet me

Bitter stream

Waking dream

Meet me in the in between

There we'll hide

There we'll hide

Hollow gorge

Steel forge

Meet my lips on foggy fjord

There we'll hide

There we'll hide

Passions produce consequence

Express true love in one sentence

Leave that to the fates and fears

Meet me in the living years

Giving up

Empty cup

Meet me where we're safe to dream

There we'll hide

There we'll hide

Finite blast

Finish fast

Meet me where we'll ever last

There we'll hide

There we'll hide

Fidelity is present tense

Indebted to the seventh sense

Let our story leave a mark

Let the next true love embark

Hi there, Dad

Hi there, Dad

I'm proud of you

What you've done

What you've been through

I search the visage of the past

It has passed, you outlast

You buried deep within my soul

There you set the Lord

Hi there, Dad

You've honored me

Your blessings there

In spite of me

You are a soft and gentle soul

And peace I see now was your goal

You left in me the best of you

Thank you, Dad for all you do!

Little peach

Why good morning, little peach!

What lessons shall I today teach?

You're my minion, I'm your Gru

Our mischief heartfelt, not thought through

Little peach, I love you so

Little peach, get up, let's go

Little peach, you're my reflection

Little peach, my pure affection

Mischief managed, cast your spell

Learn thy sight words, learn them well

You're the pupil, I'll be your eye

Together knowledge we shall spy

Little peach, I love you so

Little peach, get up, let's go

Little peach, you're my reflection

Little peach, my pure affection

You love the soft and furry things
I see in you the joy they bring
Here, let us read about their homes
It won't take long, they're little tomes

Little peach, I love you so
Little peach, get up, let's go
Little peach, you're my reflection
Little peach, my pure affection

Chapter 4: Hope

The gifts I possess

The gifts I possess are of limited capacity
Greatness demands exceptional tenacity
My knowledge is of questionable voracity
Truth a band of unending elasticity

Possessions are a burden to liberty
Wealth inversely related to civility
Enduring pain grants the soul versatility
Best played chords of elegant simplicity

Depression comes from acceptance of reality
The vibrant mind is an exceptional anomaly
Their wisdom lies in construction of a simile
Resilient metaphors, agents of our destiny

Vessels we construct are corroded by uncertainty
Faith in mankind's virtue is the ultimate absurdity
To enterprise alone is to fail most assuredly
Kind souls tend to fall while the cruel enjoy longevity

The gifts I possess are of limited capacity
Vicissitudes abound, good fortune is a scarcity
Louder is the voice of a mind in search of clarity
Left and right are stronger because of their polarity

Be yourself

It's okay to be yourself
If that is who you are
In fact, we see in time's mirror
To self the lies stretch far
We could be what we should be
If we would be true
We could see what we should see
If we'd see it through

Every moment that we breathe
A pivot point for change
Amazingly we stay the course
Despite the stings and pangs
We could reap what we should sow
If we would be sure
We could harvest in the snow
If we'd just endure

Soft we now, these gears they grind
Can we believe the way?
Trails blazed but not by we
And yet there's more to say!

We could peace what should make war

If we loosen lust's grip

We could mend life's every scar

If we'd forgiveness get

Knowing

When to speak?

To learn

To live life

When to drink?

To let go

Let life

Take these moments

See them through

Strength is measured

By what we do

Oh

Turn me in

And inside out

Turn a cry of pain

Into joy's shout

And let the rain

Let it burn and fade

Let the pain inside

Let it melt away

When to ask?

To know

To wonder why

When to think?

To laugh

Out loud

Let the bright whites

Fade to gray

Mercy proved by

What we won't do

Oh

Turn me in

And inside out

Turn a cry of pain

Into joy's shout

And let the rain

Let it burn and fade

Let the pain inside

Let it melt away

Don't-s and do-s

Don't travel down a road
If you can't go the distance
Don't boast that you will do
Then retreat in an instant
Don't make a plan in haste
You ultimately will waver
Don't jest at others' wounds
For they may be your savior
Don't meddle in affairs
Of those which aren't your making
Don't be afraid to fall
In faith there's no forsaking

A list of don't-s and do-s
Whichever you may choose
The only way to lose
Is believing you can't move

Do make your talents sweat
Your own mind must you master
Do wrestle out regret
Behold, you'll forgive faster

Do complement God's grace

By paying forward kindness

Do take the time to teach

Your learnings drive out blindness

Do make amends with haste

For bridges bring together

Do love without respect

Then any storm you'll weather

A list of don't-s and do-s

Whichever you may choose

The only way to lose

Is believing you can't move

Life

Man can't think, can drink
Life is always on the brink
Always there, that fear
That our end is drawing near

Don't look now, ask how
Ever dare to turn around
Reach higher, perspire
Pull these feet out of the mire

Stunning, endless cunning
Inching when we should be running
Letting the rhythm of a day
Get beating and swiftly dance away
Bask in the shade
Of life's ceaseless serenade
Some may dub it a charade
Embracing, retracing the parade

One thing sure, be pure
That these blessings may endure
Purity, the tree
Bearing fruits for all to see

Daring, devil sharing

Sleeping instead of preparing

Freeing the chaos of a mind

Chasing ideas, falling behind

Cosmic display

Characters all we, on the stage

Without faith, hope is betrayed

Impressing, regressing in the maze

Blurry lines

Pulled aside from time to time

Walking lines that cross the line

And there it goes again

Unnerved, up against the mouth of a mountain

Climb this hill

See the future

Make these visions blur

Blur into reality, reality

Walking apart, hand in hand

Each wrath or curse a challenge

To be overcome, overwhelmed

What world will be explored next?

Build it up

Let it fly

Make these visions blur

Blur into reality, reality

We can so we are

Conserve what we learn

Spend what we know

Live like today

Knows not tomorrow

Cast not thy net

To empty seas

Conflicts arise

Cowardice flees

We can be much

We can be more

We can give back

We can't ignore

Share what we've earned

Earn what we've shared

Spurn not the past

The future has not cared

Let not thy roots

Be thy sworn post

If so thy present

Shall be thy ghost

We can be free

We can let go

We cannot see

We all must show

Speak then the truth

May it reveal

Make thyself truth

Do not conceal

That in our weakness

In that we're strong

That we confide in

Shall be our song!

We are divine

We are assured

We are all saved

We are secured

I write

I write and write

Write some things right

And late at night

My thoughts take flight

So far above

So down below

My struggle yes

My struggle no

I write and write

Write some things right

Such lofty height

Brought low despite

The little things

Which make us wrong

Another cause

To write a song

I write and write

Write some things right

The bitter bite

When pain spawns spite

Love does not go

Away with time

That's how we know

It is divine!

Power

Power, whose essence is energy

By whose spark art thou cascaded

To the lonesome few locked out

Of great cause and purchase?

Fitting, perhaps, such impetus

Arises from that undefinable source

From which no traveler may confess

Despite treading deep through

Entanglements of her unseen will

Surreal as our sundry devotions manifest

They be all rooted in fertile soil of desire

Passion is the foundation of all achievement

And divers drivers of unequivocal conviction

Bare painful their equilibrium and balance

Such that we may understand

In the compression of expanding time

The accomplishments of quantum oscillations

Of which we all be born and we all return

Relief of faith

Take these my eyes
That I may see
Grant me the insight
Of infinity

Block out my fear
That I may shield
Unmask and reveal
This hurt I've concealed

The further we stretch
Our bones will reverse
Reciting our schemes
Chapter and verse

Now comes the moment
To sink or swim
Haplessly floating
On temporal winds

Fuse hope and peace
My faith implores
Make joy my marrow
Love's pure hope restore!

As much

As much as we lose, there's more we can gain
Some of it joy, some of it pain
As much as we clean, there's always a stain
Do it by faith or do it in vain

As much as we sing, there's more to be heard
Truth speaks plainly, never obscured
As much as we struggle, we are assured
One act absorbed all we deserve

As much as we seek, there's more we can see
Some lose their way, some never be
As much as we deny eternity
Cynics and shackles, neither will free

Try me

Throw me left, throw me right

Think I have no inner will to fight?

Try me, I say try me, try me!

Toss me down, toss me up

Think that I've thought of giving up?

Try me, I say try me, try me!

Special characters, I'm not

Baneful handles not for me

Painful step ladders, I tread

Wondrous sea, anonymity

Knock me down, knock me out

Think this round, this is a bout

Try me, I say try me, try me!

Weary sleep

Every night I lay my head
Gently to the stony depth
Hold my breath, for what's next
Pull my dreams from daily wrecks

Sometimes evenings come too fast
Stories, visions blur and blast
Broken bonds like bones in cast
Let this conscience rest at last

Chew on comfort, sweet cigar
Imagination's door ajar
Light the wick, sleep isn't far
Let the dark blot out these scars

Pull me apart

Pull me apart
Cut me in two
Every day changing
Changing for you
Oh yeah

Appointed time
Shedding our fear
Ashes erasing
Stand in the clear
Oh yeah

Climb out of the horizon
Hold the line
Fall then rise on thy orison
Living vine

Into the cold
Beneath the skin
Unleash the terror
Lurking within
Oh yeah

Confront and learn

Freedom must bleed

Vanity's mirror

Flesh will concede

Oh yeah

Climb out of the horizon

Hold the line

Fall then rise on thy orison

Living vine

Faint glow

Faint glow swallowed by deep horizon

As sail we, across teeming seas

What creatures stir beneath

These emerald waves?

Onward, pressed we by

Hoarse and fervent commandment

Peace cometh from the bondage of our faith

Together we row and hoist and veer

Against rupturing tides and

Seductive breeze

Look ye on these bruised souls

Ceaselessly flirting with starvation

Or those diseases plucked from rot

And sundry deprivations

For she, who hides beyond horizon

We travail and persevere such

Intolerable conditions

All these sufferings will pale

Upon her wellspring of youth and vitality

Reflecting grace

Grace, the conscious application of perpetual, unmerited mercy

Make me thy student

Grace, the love which persists through scorn and pitiless rebuke

Pluck the splinters from my spirit

As we traverse parched grounds of apathy

Mocked by the oases of ungrounded hope

My lips thirst for the clear waters of her majesty's bounty

Grace, that unseen force which moves soul and nation

Fit me with perspective's lens

Grace, as immovable as thy purpose immutable

Dull the barbs of my youth

A beast's affections are no more permanent than they are transcendent

Kneel before the Mother of humankind's most potent inspirations

My body, mind, and spirit seem endlessly for her communion

Just outside

When the great steal from small

They are not great at all

When the small steal from great

Reciprocate hate

Sin crafts only sinful

An evil heart, its core

Convincing small they're nothing

Convincing great they're more

One Judge awaits them, just outside

The One to end the war

One Judge awaits them, just outside

The One opens the door

Intricate

Sway with the breezes

Many winds of wild blow

Grip, don't hold

Grip, don't hold

Dance with the darkness

Carving stories in snow

Slip, don't fall

Slip, don't fall

Everything is intricate

Delicate and pure

For those who depart

Never will return

Everything is intricate

Penitents endure

Wise souls, boldly reticent

Learning from their scars

Let me ask

Let me ask you just one thing
If you could spare the time
Most want to hear themselves sing
Likewise, I'm singing mine

Let me ask you just one thing
As day turns night turns day
Simple answers often bring
Great strength, great minds belay

Tarried have I, up till now
To ask you just one thing
Don't ask me, I don't know how
Except I love to sing!

Here's the question, to be asked
I've thought it through and through
Out now with it, out at last!
Do you inspire you?

The haze

The haze of distant realities

Raised up and rooted on soft quartz

Bright, luminous waves, diamond-tipped

Crashing serenely and without sound

Hitherto unexplored, unexplained

Forgotten past, forever stained

The heat of a midsummer's evening

Radiant bliss, driving to cool water

Bold, inspired tranquility, solitude

Spread amongst these restful masses

Wanting not, willing yet

Affixing calm melodies to their shoals

Ex nihilo

No thing comes from nothing
Yet some thing somehow did
To boldly challenge status quo
Is what this world forbids
Asking the right questions
Prove answers in themselves
Our rhetoric, such endless loops
Recursing through our cells

No thing comes from nothing
Can science contradict?
The evil in our best exists!
And thus, the atom split
Vessels of the brightest
Have dimmed our history
Minds of titans, motives of man
Betrayal, treachery!

No thing comes from nothing
Equations don't perceive
The command of a newborn's eyes
No device can conceive

There is no space or time
Beyond the shell of glass
The farther out we cast our gaze
The less our knowledge lasts

No thing comes from nothing
We learn to prove we're wrong
Watch nature thwart and falsify
So, challenge and be strong!
All we've ever studied
All gains will sum to naught
Our creations turn creation
Against all that we've wrought

No thing comes from nothing
A void itself, a thing
To fill a space that is not there
Expansion, but a dream!
Debating, such a chore
Hostility, expect
Their narrative is well rehearsed
There is no win to get

No thing comes from nothing

This truth is all we need

The lofty grandeur of the learned

Mere vainglory and greed

Our faith is more precious

Than all the books of men

A friend who loves us more than us

Who saves us from our sin

Some thing sang to nothing

And from His song we're born

His melody made space and time

We from His fabric torn

Popular, He is not

Although He made all things

Ex Nihilo, creation's song

All those with joy doth sing!

Till you're dead

This is what you'll do till dead

Get out there living

Outside your head

Are you the thing from where you're from?

What spiteful thing

Have you become?

This is what you'll be till dead

A thing worth being

Not what you dread

You want the grace, so lose the blame

Freedom awaits

Invoke his name

This is what you'll do till dead

Rest with forgiveness

On mercy's bed

Unsatisfied by lowly things

Release your pride

See what love brings

I find myself

I find myself without a word
To tame this aching mood
Supposing that I had this gift
No wait, that is absurd

I'm not the kind of eloquence
That moves a mortal soul
Supposing that I had this gift
I certainly use this sense

If a million years existed
To solve endless riddles
Supposing that I had this gift
I'd be not resisted

True entertainer

Style, elusive

Yet laid bare

For when we see it

We all stare

And for a moment

Maybe two

We think of us

As being you

There you are

Upon a stage

Wrestling out

Converting rage

Perhaps in darkness

There be joy

But we both know

This little boy

Who leapt upon

A world of ills

And set to mind

A young man's will?

From murky depth

And hazy highs

From meekness

Your strength realized

Voices

Struggle is the burden of the fit
Strength is something earned, not a gift
So many, and they won't back down
In the cacophony I'm drowned

Fearful we, evaluating odds
Sate our minds, pretending we be gods
Raise the volume of contention
Slain are we by our inventions

Voices, voices coloring our world
Brilliant panacea where ideas are unfurled
Voices, voices making up our minds
The louder they are, the more likely they are blind

Wandering, along the winding trails
Upon which premise shall we prevail?
Illness, a reason to be meek
Patience, a reason not to speak

Sorrow is renewing to the heart

Tears are cleansing, granting a fresh start

Scattered, to four corners driven

This gospel, we are forgiven!

Voices, voices make or break our joy

Hope a faithful solider, by pain's command deployed

Voices, voices let us speak as one

May we all enjoy the peace, as the war's already won

In the mix

Ride the uplift

As the gears grind

Get up above and see the signs

Nothing's waiting

For an answer

It's up to you to use your time

Running away may slow it down

But where you run it hunts you down

Stop the talking

Turn to action

Make more excuses and decline

Climb the ladder

It'll be long

All good things come from sweat and time

Keeping the lies will bind you down

Let go of pride before you drown

Make some magic

Turn the light on

Full life is full of love and pain

Let the past go

May new dreams rise

Answers are there and yours to find

Sober moments

Sober moments follow bliss
This pain inside will subsist
On little cuts, which scrape a vein
On self-pity I am sustained

Scraps of time make up my life
Memories of strain and strife
Nearly all were of my making
I've gone far for all my faking

Dim the lights within my mind
I would forgive, if I were kind
All I see is madness, darkness
How can weakness lead to progress?

Sober moments follow bliss
Depressed, a force I can't resist
I'll lay my soul upon the altar
By faith alone, I will not falter

Tell me a good story

Tell me a good story, one I'll understand
Don't make it long and tedious
For that I cannot stand

Horror won't appease me, I've had my fill of bleak
Don't bother with a comedy
They leave me incomplete

Ironies, overdone. An independent theme
Perhaps shrouded in mystery
Where none is what it seems

Then again, I wonder, if that would fit the bill
Are mysteries the remedies?
Or would I hunger still?

Tell me a good story, that one command is clear
Craft characters I'll love and hate
Ensure I'll hold them dear

Romance pure is subtle, let true love bloom in time

Blend pain and pleasure equally

A hurried work a crime

Action clearly something for quickening the pace

Brave hero fighting tyranny

On Earth or outer space

Intrepid my desire to lose myself in prose

Truths hidden in creative ways

No single story knows

Stay with us

We are walking, take our hand
Look ahead, the promised land
You hit a snag, tripped a snare
Know that we are always there

Stay with us
For one more night
Stay with us
All is alright

If you hold, to who you are
You'll see so clear, see so far
Let it go, start to dream
Sometimes it is what it seems

Stay with us
For one more night
Stay with us
All is alright

We will worship, sing a song

Kindness helps you get along

You make the place, you make home

Let love touch everything you own

Stay with us

For one more night

Stay with us

All is alright

It's not that difficult, really

Something as simple as a smile
Will make a blue day green
If green is a color of contentment
I suppose that's what I mean

One need not lean on intellect
To shape simple, profound
Unabashedly not my implement
On the beach progress is browned

Discovery is manifest
So says the open mind
Acquaintances are easy to deceive
Especially if they're blind

Repetition is mastery
But who has time for that?
Fitness to task a sign of time ill spent
Lean today, tomorrow fat

It's not that difficult, really
To eat, drink and … you know
Materiality of our purpose
To find a good place to go

Final thoughts

What are your final thoughts?
If you could speak them now
What did your life sum up to?
What brought you low, high, proud?

Would you bless the days you had?
Or curse the life short lived?
Had you had some more time
What is it that you'd give?

Did you make it on your own?
Is someone worth a mention?
What lies do you yet cling?
So cold are our inventions

Did you propagate your seed?
The last one of your kind?
These are your final thoughts
Let truth bleed from your mind

Ex nihilo you came
Nihil est will you go?
Speak loudly and proclaim
Let earth and heavens know

Clouding

Break above the silky, bright barrier

Smooth ripples and soft curves

Vast sheets of ivory, stretched to turquoise horizon

Subtle currents in motion

Shifting pristine gasses, navigating new destinations

A canvas for melodious dreams

Upon which we may each reflect

In these heavens there is no distress

Release all angst and tensions in this space

We have barely risen, and so much has changed

No striking verse or phrase

Can connect eye to mind

Such beauty must be excited on one's own nerve

And with the faith in minority

We can share in collective wisdom there found

Prime

Define a number, two by two

Not like that, please

Think it through

Make a number that is fun

Divide by self

And only one

What kind of number would that be?

Now calculate

Go one, two, three

Assign this number a unique name

Make it special

It's not lame

This number can hold either sign

Remember that and

Make it prime

My oh my

My prose has lows
And highs, I suppose
The more that I explore
The more I am exposed

In the center of the tangle
Lacerating bladed grasses
I want me some attention
But I shy me from the masses

My poems have pride
And shame I cannot hide
The more I attempt
The more I can confide

On a balmy summer evening
Inspiration strikes, I'm bleeding
I have complete attention
There's nothing else I'm needing

Mountain

The mountain shall not yield
To the winds, which warp the field
The mountain shall not bend
To the storms, which will descend

Conception from so long ago
Eternal life in their shadow
The pride and joy of poets' pens
How wondrous are pristine mountains

And if the mountain fall
Be it the downfall of us all
Though acid rains they may erode
A mountain's core cannot corrode

High upon their snowy peak
There is no place there for the weak
But for the few that there survive
Through every season will they thrive

Artistic expression

Artistic expression

Best sprinkled with depression

Young ones learn this lesson

Sadness, a valuable possession

Artistic expression

An endless strained confession

Repetition the obsession

Now, let us have another session

Artistic expression

Rehearsing indiscretion

Confirming the impression

Of the thriving in transgression

Save

Compulsory the verses

Each pore of mine an open door

Through which the trivial and profound

Release in slow beads of inspiration

Lenses each, mirrors same

Bundled conduit, steaming cells

Energy and light pervade

Synapses unleashed, unapologetic

Explore as you may, and I may follow

Glorious tutor in my youth

Lift my feet off cracked, dry earth

Escape me to thy fields, fertility

Ascend as steam through the depths

Release power and conviction

Thou art in my charge, savage

My command is to graciously heal

Save me and so be saved

What will you make?

Take your day, a busy day
Running in so many ways
What did you learn?
What did you make?

Take your night, a quiet night
No time now to make it right
What will you think?
What will you make?

Every day is ordinary
Until you choose it not to be
What will you make?
Go tell your story

Take this hour, a burning hour
Stretch thy fingers, emit thy power!
You will create
What did you make?

Art

Expressionless the canvas that stares blankly at the eyes

Of the artist trying to express what others can't surmise

Every stroke upon the canvas is a story that gives rise

To the debt paid to the reaper of a billion broken lives

Without pain no mercy, and without pride no fear

Does the artist's creature capture that which others hold so dear?

The price for selfish action is a bill paid in arrears

A good artist knows to put below all else but their career

There is ceaseless saturation in the artist's maddened mind

For to paint a painful picture means to leave all hope behind

But there is a contradiction, and no artist should be blind

That the human need is joy and from the darkness we unbind

Thus, a work of art is broken and completely
  incomplete

If there is no other ending than the ending of heart's
  beat

And the canvas once so blank now holds a message
  so concrete

Do not let go of the simple things that make our lives
  complete

Angel

A world away, an angel lay
Her broken wings had blown away
She rested on the silky green
Shadowed by a mountain stream

No one there to stay her pain
The angel wrestled with her faith
For she had lived true to the light
And now befell to blistering blithe

This little angel, oh so pure
How much more can she endure?
So many cries did she respond
Yet here she suffered all alone

A stranger came across her path
And saw her ravaged by God's wrath
In his hands, he held the keys
For he had found her angel wings

He held her gently while she wept
The secret of her wings he kept
And as they lay, he fell in love
With this broken angel from above

Her wings recovered and did mend
The stranger took her by the hand
He asked that she remember this
She kissed him with her angel lips

She pressed his hands upon her heart
He felt the warmth and fell apart
Such grace and strength, it overwhelmed
And to her eyes he was compelled

She knew she could not stay below
Her home, the heavens far above
But in his eyes, she saw a pearl
He did not belong to this world

And so she spread her crystal wings
Her flawless voice began to sing
The earth around began to shake
An angel's love did new wings make

And in the stars their tale stored
For those below when hope seems lore
A message to the universe
An angel's kiss does death reverse

A beach

Take these little waves of sand
They be small, but they be grand
Formed by wind's delicate hand
Making little waves of sand

Take these vast and rolling dunes
They be to the tide immune
Treasures stored like ancient ruins
Hidden in the rolling dunes

Take these little wandering prints
They be tokens of time spent
Flocks of joy they represent
In these little wandering prints

Take these deep and green lagoons
They be here, but be gone soon
Hapless they against the moon
Deep and green are these lagoons

Desert flower

Desert flower come to bloom

Moments come and go so soon

As the rains go, so do you

Survive another season

River crystal running wild

I need you like a mother's child

Our temple shall be undefiled

Seek a greater reason

Performs

See how the world performs, she performs, she
   performs

Like a fluid on stage standing up as the crowd sits
   still

Silence before the storm, every detail in her arms

See how she performs, she performs, she performs

Who are we to say what she abhors?

In her barren womb was all life borne

She cares not for morality

In her eyes, spirituality

She how the world performs, she performs, she
   performs

Like the lightning of a daydream while the dark
   clouds thunder share

Rain to wet the parched throats just before, just
   before

She how the world performs, she performs, she
   performs

Who are we to say what she abhors?

In her barren womb was all life borne

She cares not for morality

In her eyes, spirituality

Free man

A free man writes because he's free
Enjoying peace, her tranquility
A sad man writes because he's bound
To lofty thoughts glued to the ground

I am free, I am free
Set me free, set me free
I am free, I am free
Free man

A cruel man writes because he's scared
Upon dark altar, his soul is bared
A lost man writes because he's trained
That hope and faith are sullied, stained

I am free, I am free
Set me free, set me free
I am free, I am free
Free man

A strong man writes because he's proud

Man's vanity is a blinding shroud

A weak man writes because he's free

And this is God's great subtlety

I am free, I am free

Set me free, set me free

I am free, I am free

Free man

Winter

Street lights spill on untouched snow

Shadows, crisp and clean

Carolers to the weary sing

All is all a dream

Warming smells of pine and birch

Flames lick air and dance

Wreaths of green on every door

Winter, sweet romance

Many bodes, coats, and gloves

Smiling as they maze

Children sense the sweet surprise

Brief be their holidays

Stories, legends, tales of olde

Gather all ye round

Sleep we cannot till we hear

Good tidings touch the ground

Waterfall

Patient force to move thee mountains

Predict thee not

For thou art motion

Endless ways, thy shifting form

Calculation not thy norm

Thy music rest, harmony peace

Regardless if shallow or deep

To thy means, submit our days

Navigating all thy ways

Within thy bosom life and flesh

To nothing would thy will contest

Speak ye to these muted ears

Create thee, free thee, many fears

Gods could not withstand thy force

And from our hearts could not divorce

What thy shape means to our minds

Be thy endless, wax divine

Kingmaker

Gliding just above the turquoise water
Pad foot in the forest, chasing hunger
Wrapped around the unsuspecting victim
Wonders great and small, all made by Him

Kingmaker, touched the depths
Abode of truth, of light, of breath
Kingmaker, spoke the Word
Obeyed the waters, heavens, earth

Stretching far to reach into a sapling
Warning troublemakers, vicious rattling
Harvesting a bounty for long winter
Live by out maneuvering the sprinter

Kingmaker, prominence
Bound hemispheres, poles opposites
Kingmaker, promises
Make fear and joy synonymous

Feast upon the crumbs from over feeding

Nourishment comes from another's bleeding

Deep below the surface, luminescence

Blending to avoid, sweet evanescence

Kingmaker, touched the depths

Abode of truth, of light, of breath

Kingmaker, spoke the Word

Obeyed the waters, heavens, earth

Epilogue

Journey

Pale faces, scarlet coated

Some lack substance, others bloated

Ceaseless groans, decay and blight

The bright of day a dim twilight

Anger heightened, falling embers

Skies went black one cold December

An irony in season giving

A maddened world sought nothing living

Sirens blaring, masses scatter

No soul knew what was the matter

As chaos gripped charmed finger's hand

"Launch them all!" was the command

Trails blazing, brilliant flashes

Converting all our work to ashes

In the most remote of places

Survived some in their buried spaces

Throats of wanting, resource draining
Ex terra came forth the changelings
What had they been before the storm?
What would they be within the swarm?

Falling quickly, disease spreading
Survivor's footsteps lightly treading
Very few could play the board
Falling prey to roaming hordes

Beasts above, bad dreams below
Thick coats adorned to battle snow
The earth suspended, brutal winter
Lock tight thy doors or become dinner

A boy survived, his sister too
Their parents died to see them through
They made a home in thick, dark wood
Deep in a cave as though they should

Brother younger, sister older
She'd often weep, he'd often hold her
Their lessons learned before their teens
That living men are ruthless, mean

In hiding these young tots were schooled
To read, to hide, to not be fooled
Deceit and hunger ruled the day
Their parents nightly with them prayed

Eve the girl born to the madness
In her burned more rage than sadness
Her brother Peter came years after
He was disposed to joy and laughter

Their parents toiled to keep them safe
By more than food and water, faith
They'd often sing redemption songs
The days grew dark, the night grew long

In absentia, cold and frightened
These two children's fear was heightened
Their parents drew death's beasts away
Their children would live one more day

Each day precious, none for granted
Young Eve's seal of strength implanted
She would lead, protect her brother
For her father, for his mother

Each day painful, constant sadness
Young Pete's soul was touched with madness
Remembering his mother's screaming
While awake or while he's dreaming

First came water, then came eating
Foodstuffs were quickly depleting
Eve grew bolder, searching farther
Witnessing men for meal, slaughter

Eve kept working, Pete was failing
Late at night she'd hear him wailing
Her bitterness gave way to thriving
She learned life meant more than surviving

Days spent reading, through books taken
From a world truth had forsaken
But with the days of purposed time
Pete found his home close by Eve's side

Eve his leader, Pete grew stronger
His pain reminder, not controller
They made their way west through the wood
Adept at sneaking, as they should

One cool morning, on misty hill
Just after dawn came forth a shrill
That high-pitched squeal which trailed death
The children ran till out of breath

Closing rapid, beasts gone rabid
Through a gulch the children scrambled
Grasping wildly, up wetted stones
A maneuver which the dead can't clone

Rotted clutches, safety nearing
Eve and Pete climbed to a clearing
Staring down at their escaping
Moaning groaning jaws, and scraping

Sullen sockets, glazed whitened orbs
All evils of the world absorbed
These mindless things, they mutants be
Reflecting our sins outwardly

Eve found a place, Pete made it safe
They'd aged eight years between the space
A home built far up in the trees
Obscured from view by the dense leaves

One escape route, one passage in
A temperate world within their den
They lived by day and hid by night
Three years did pass without a fight

They'd see some come, they'd see all go
As frequently the dead would show
Some bands of men, some single strands
No peace be found on shifting sands

Eve was lovely, Pete was ruddy
Their countenance remained unsullied
Yet Pete held sorrow in his eyes
Trapped deep inside throughout his life

Eve's rich black hair had silver streaks
Much like the dirt on her white cheeks
Her eyes were green, her brow cunning
She was as fierce as she was stunning

Pete's head a mop of curly brown
His skin was dark, his body sound
Muscles he wore, more for bluffing
He was gentle, he was loving

Late one night smoke filled the trees
And with the wind they had to flee
Marauding bands of warring tribes
Turned quiet wood to raging pyre

The world still like it was before
Peace always finds a path to war
Eve and Pete raced through the evening
To each other's side were clinging

Daylight saw they made it safely
They faced death, they faced it bravely
Biding time within a gully
Washing off their clothes so bloody

They forged a plan, from nerves of steel
As if from heaven it was revealed
They'd travel light, by cloak and hood
And cling to shadows as they should

The season spring, they could not know
For every footstep tread through snow
Without harm they sustained plenty
Genteel marauders in their twenties

Endless peaks gave way to plains
An endless landscape free from stains
There were no fires, no glows, no stakes
Where had they come, what was this place?

They were exposed, they weren't afraid
For they knew death, the games he played
Eve called Pete close to her side
She said, "Look there, have my eyes lied?"

For what she saw, and Pete did too
A village out from green plains grew
"We must proceed," Pete said so firmly
Eve agreed, then they both hurried

A feeling Pete and Eve knew well
This place was far, so far from hell
They approached, lowered their hoods
Broadcast peace as though they should

The new world had lost trust of men
Oh, depths of sin when there's no sin!
Buildings dark wood, sturdily made
Appearing aged by time, then saved

The streets of packed sand well maintained
No trace of death, no black blood stains
Small packs of people hurried by
Well dressed, well kept, stood side by side

Their faces covered by thick veils
Their robes were white and flowed like sails
They did not speed, they did not slow
But all they knew just where to go

Each one's motions mimicked marching
As to orders none were barking
Commands lingered in silent air
All people led by one not there

Quiet, calm the masses wandered
Eve and Pete stood, studied, pondered
Slowly walking through the city
Eve and Pete sought out a friendly

Towards the far end of the village
Stood a sign with vibrant visage
An old man's face with youthful cheer
Below his glow three words spelled clear

Emphatic print a surety
"Security through Purity"
Adjacent to the sign a door
Tall, bright and red, slightly ajar

"Is this the place to which we're led?"
Asked Pete, as if inside Eve's head
"This omen may be evil, may be good"
Cautious each, as though they should

Clutching blades they entered slowly
Laughter echoed down the hallway
Long and straight the dim lit passage
Lined with ornate goblets, glasses

"Come now, come now," arose soft voice
As if to leave them but one choice
Damp brick arch the separation
Some new thing their destination

Circular the spacious chamber
Lined with maces, mauls and sabers
Firelight hanging from chain-linked steel
Wet gray stone walls shone like eels

A warming red glow lit this space

And fell upon the old man's face

Just like the painting back outside

His countenance was soft and kind

Upon a royal's chair he perched

While two guards by his side did lurch

Two hulking things in crimson gowns

With hidden eyes that stared them down

The large room suddenly felt so small

Their destiny could not forestall

For something larger was at play

This town was purposed in their way

Gray hair untamed with wild eyes blue

The old man spoke as if he knew

"You have arrived out of the wild,"

His eyes danced like those of a child

"This town is Sidon, I am Tyre,

All living offered solace here"

He studied them with brilliant eyes

As if he could see through man's lies

Unlike the people in the town
Tyre wore no veil, no flowing gown
His clothing dusty, one time black
With no desire to have it back

"We've wandered for so many years,"
Eve motioned forward, engaged Tyre
"My name is Eve, his name is Pete,
We've traveled far on just our feet"

"Indeed," Tyre said with wondrous gaze
"We've been watching you both for days"
Pete and Eve exchanged a glance
This meeting certainly not by chance

"We have survived," Eve said plainly
"We have endured our trials bravely"
Silence lingered for a moment
In Eve's head re-ran Tyre's slogan

Tyre's eyes danced between his guests
Patience commands one's confidence
"We seek a place to call our home,
To rebuild, repair, stone by stone"

Eve turned back, saw Pete's approval

Their case made, now Tyre's reproval

Tyre's smile widened but his eyes narrowed

His gaze into their hearts burrowed

"The souls I've saved struggled, endured

They knew disease, I knew the cure

I showed mercy, turned none away

All illness purged for those who stayed"

"Our home is safe and free from rot

It is secure, free from onslaught

"But what I offer is not free,

The price is your identity"

Eve three steps back, her brother four

So far away was the front door

"What does that mean? What do you want?"

Eve felt Tyre in her spirit haunt

"Yet I am puzzled by one thing"

Tyre answered Eve not, he was king

"Your will and wit have clarity

No trace in you my remedy"

The hulking beasts moved from Tyre's side

Keeping Eve and Pete inside

Sister, brother understanding

What this man before them planning

They weren't meant for safe arrival

Crime committed, their survival

A faceless walker was their fate

Eve shrugged off fear to clearly state

"You have not saved a living breath,

Instead you have perfected death!"

With this the old man's face turned sour

How dare the feeble mock his power

His eyes rolled back, turned white and pale

His skin transformed to ash-gray scales

His dusty black suit fell to ground

Replaced at once by maroon gown

Eve felt a coldness grow inside her

Before her stood the Pale Rider

She learned this name from her mother

Kept it hidden from her brother

Eve had dismissed the explanation
Angel's heralding man's damnation
Her parents would pray every night
They claimed they missed rapturous light

Hence Eve was born when doomsday fell
This Earth, to her, persistent hell
She'd seen the acts of living men
No demons oversaw their sins

Yet long ago, deep in a cave
Her brother's love did each they save
And this was manifestly clear
She'd not let her brother die here

Eve's reflection turned to action
Buying time through a distraction
"I've learned of you, I know your name
This Earth is yours and ours the same!"

With this Tyre's dead eyes turned to Eve
His grave-borne face showed disbelief
Pete drew his blade, Eve held him back
No mortal thing could this attack

"Divine the judgment of mankind
This world for one thousand years mine
They had their chance to change, repent
And yet they mocked the one He sent"

Tyre spoke these words, moved not his lips
He hovered there, dust 'round him wisped
"I know your name, now I believe"
Eve knew the truth now finally

He knew she knew, that she was sure
He can't unseal what's not impure
For in this plane men may yet choose
To serve death's will or be set loose

The world before the rapturous light
Man's time was short to live upright
The after-world lifetimes a sieve
There is no death, for death now lived

"You speak the truth, I can't coerce
The choice is yours, serve or traverse
But if you leave, please don't forget
One thousand years you'll flee torment"

"Until the final judgment comes
You'll live under a setting sun
My minions span most of the earth
No home is yours, no place of mirth"

Pete stepped to Eve, he knew their path
They'd wander on and face death's wrath
A little smile across his face
He felt Eve's faith, he felt true grace

"Let us go," Pete so demanded
Tyre agreed as so commanded
Tyre's hulking beasts drew to his side
Revealing a dim light outside

Before their eyes Tyre transformed back
To the old man, suit dusty, black
"Be on your way, may you return
I'll enjoy as both you burn"

They wandered out to after world
This little boy, this little girl
A thousand years to seek the good
Side by side just as they should

Made in the USA
Las Vegas, NV
07 August 2021

27733770R00164